UP CLOSE
AND
PERSONAL

UP CLOSE AND PERSONAL

ROY TSCHUDY

authorHOUSE®

AuthorHouse™
1663 Liberty Drive
Bloomington, IN 47403
www.authorhouse.com
Phone: 1-800-839-8640

Published by AuthorHouse   03/15/2012

ISBN: 978-1-4685-4226-4 (sc)
ISBN: 978-1-4685-4225-7 (e)

Library of Congress Control Number: 2012901182

Any people depicted in stock imagery provided by Thinkstock are models, and such images are being used for illustrative purposes only.
Certain stock imagery © Thinkstock.

This book is printed on acid-free paper.

Because of the dynamic nature of the Internet, any web addresses or links contained in this book may have changed since publication and may no longer be valid. The views expressed in this work are solely those of the author and do not necessarily reflect the views of the publisher, and the publisher hereby disclaims any responsibility for them.

You make a living by what you get
You make a life by what you give.
. . . Sir Winston Churchill
British Politician
(1874-1965)

Life, Made A Couple, Took Some, Saved A Few

FORWARD

I first met Roy Tschudy when we both worked in Suffern High School which is located in Rockland County, New York. He worked as a security officer, and I served in a variety of capacities Teacher, Administrator, and Summer School Principal. Roy exuded family values, he was a trusted friend, confidant, loyal, dedicated and committed to protecting all the members of the Suffern High School family. Roy Tschudy is a man of deep conviction, life to him is either black or white, right or wrong, there is no grey area in between.

I always thought of Roy as being an Everyman—an "average Joe" preoccupied with taking care of his family, dealing with some serious war-related health issues, and making it though the day with an affable demeanor and smile on his face. "Up Close and Personal" reveals the truly heroic person he is. In a series of poignant vignettes. The reader experiences the fear and anguish of the Vietnam front lines, the ongoing emotional turmoil faced by Vietnam Vets, a day in the life of a New York City cop, and last but not least, fond family memories, and a man's best friend named Sammy.

America was shaped by young men and women like Roy Tschudy who lived in big cities throughout our country, many in single parent families, who answered their country's call to defend liberty and freedom throughout the world. Roy may have left Vietnam, but Vietnam never left him, it was an experience that left him emotionally and physically scarred for the rest of his life,—Finding solace in his family, friends and close acquaintances. "Up Close and Personal" offers a glimpse into the life of a true hero, who has never stopped believing that "you make a living by what you get, and you make a life by what you give."

Phil Tisi

THE LONGEST NIGHT
THE SHORTEST NIGHT
A TRIBUTE TO A FALLEN BROTHER

1969

SGT. DEWITT STUDWAY

THE LONGEST NIGHT THE SHORTEST NIGHT

TRIBUTE TO A FALLEN BROTHER

I was all of 18 years when I was shipped off to Vietnam in January 1968. The U.S.S. Upshur was a Navy troop carrier ship that would take my company, the 271st Aviation Assault Helicopter Unit across the Pacific Ocean to South East Asia. It took thirty day's to do so, and not one of us ever realized just how vast the ocean really was.

We were located in the bow of the ship (Front end) stacked six high, one bed atop of another "Grab a top bunk!" my friend Dewitt yelled to me, "Crap on that! I'll fall out of the bunk at night and get killed before I even get to Nam." Once again, Dewitt said "Trust me, hurry up and grab a top one," as he himself scrambled up to a top bunk directly opposite the other stack of beds. "What the hell," I thought to myself and dutifully climbed up and up to what I was certain was going to be my undoing. "You'll see, you'll see" he said to me, "Yeah I'll see alright" I shot back, "I'll see the floor of this ship when I come crashing down at night." Dewitt just laughed and shook his head slowly.

The two of us were friends, admittedly, not best friends, but friends just the same. As we both learned in our very first conversation together, Dewitt had joined the Army on the same exact date as I had, funny as it seemed, that was probably the only thing we had in common. Dewitt was twenty years old; a light skinned African American, and married with a baby daughter. He hailed from a small town in Mississippi where he was born and raised. Dewitt was a likeable fella who was quiet and soft spoken; he seemed more mature than most of us at that time. He was also a skilled mechanic who was promoted to Sergeant and put in charge of the company motor pool (Army Vehicles) probably not just for his skills, but also because of his likeability.

I, on the other hand, was SP/4 E-4 in rank and was soon to discover what my duties would be upon my arrival in Nam. I was an eighteen year old white kid from the Bronx N.Y., growing up in the housing projects, raised along with two sisters by my Mom. My Dad had passed away when I was five years old, the girls were Holly seven years and Lennore who was all of four years of age.

"Splat! Aarrph! Splat! Splat!," "What the hell? It was our first night out at sea on the ship; we were all hunkered down in our bunks for the night when the good old Upshur ran into a few ocean swells. Well that sound I quickly learned was from a few of the guy's who became green around the gills and began puking from the side of their beds. The unlucky souls who found themselves on the lower half of the stack of beds were now getting a bath of vomit from the above troops. As I was gazing over and around this chaos, I heard a loud, but subtle "AHEM." It was Dewitt, propped up on his elbow and looking me directly in the eye with a cocky smile on his face.

Roy enroute
to Nam

A few buddies on
board the Upshur

I mouthed the words "THANK YOU" very s-l-o-w-l-y and with much appreciation, Dewitt nodded, laid his head back on the pillow and fell back to sleep. I remember this as if it were yesterday.

Thirty day's later; we disembarked from the Upshur (Good Riddance!) in the Mekong Delta Vietnam. We were then to be flown to our base camp approximately seventy miles south of Saigon; the name of that base was Cantho. The date was January 31st 1968, for the un-informed, this is the day of the Vietnamese New Year, TET. The North Vietnamese Army (NVA) in conjunction with the local militia (Vietcong) had planned, and acted upon a strategic surprise attack on all of the major cities, villages, and towns through out all of Vietnam. Saigon, the major city in the south suffered devastating losses, the enemy was eventually beaten back and although we didn't know it at the time, the tide of the war was changing, and changing fast. Right smack in the middle of this I reflected to myself, "Self, this is a fine way to be greeted, I deeply appreciate this hospitality." Thankfully, we survived our "WELCOME GREETING," in fact, one of my buddies Gene Kramer, stated to another friend of ours Rich Radowick and myself, "HOLY SHIT, if we made it through this; we gotta make it through the year!"

Once things bean to settle down a bit at Cantho, our company, the 271st went about its tasks, day and night, seven days a week. War is not a movie, no commercials with few breaks in between. The C.O. directed that a company day room be built on our base camp and one of my job functions became head of entertainment. On a weekly basis, I would fly to Saigon and "PROCURE" odds and ends for our company and the troops. Five nights per week I was assigned to perimeter guard duty, out past the flight line near the elephant grass in a bunker system. These consisted of twelve bunkers stretching along the length of that flight line with the largest of them in the middle. This was the command bunker, this bunker had distinct advantages in that it contained six soldiers and had a protective roof made of additional sandbags. Last, but certainly not least, it had an M-60 machine gun mounted and pointed directly at where, "Charlie" might come, if indeed he came at all. The other remaining bunkers held two men apiece, were only stacked five sandbags high, and yeah, no roof, no cover, if it rained (And boy did it ever during monsoon season!) tough cookies for you, Xin Loi! Every now and then Dewitt would be the Sgt. of the guard for the night, lucky for me because he always made sure that I was in the command bunker with him.

Fast forward, Friday, January. 11, 1969. Dewitt and a few of the guys were heading over to an area on the base that served cold beer and halfway (AND I DO MEAN HALFWAY) decent food. Dewitt was going back "TO THE WORLD" on Monday, his one year tour was almost completed, I on the other hand volunteered to remain in Nam for an extra month so as receive an early out. Any soldier returning from Vietnam with five months or less remaining on their service time would be discharged, for me it was a no brainer. I would gladly spend one additional month in Nam as opposed to six months at some Fort in the states. Dewitt and I stopped to chat for a minute or so, "Hey short timer, congratulations man, goin home." He smiled and gave a quick laugh, "Yeah baby, goin home, I can't wait to see my wife and little girl, everyone." I asked if he planned on working as a mechanic back at home, and he replied that there was not much work where he lived. He went on to say that the Army had been good to him so he was going to re-enlist and make it a career; another plus that he was receiving was a promotion to staff sergeant as well. I was happy for him because he was a good dude and deserved it. I said that I would see him tonight because we were both assigned to perimeter guard duty "Sure enough" he replied before hurrying off to catch up with the guys.

That evening as we formed up prior to heading out to our posts I was surprised to see that Dewitt was not the Sgt. of the guard; instead some "Newbie" with clean fresh olive drab fatigues was now in charge for the night. "Crap," I thought to myself, it's raining and I'm gonna be stuck in some little pillbox for a long, long night. Ah, but lady luck intervened and lo and behold Roy boy was indeed in the big one, yeah baby! The next day I found out why my man Dewitt was not present for guard duty. It seems that he and the boys celebrated a tad too much, and since Dewitt was a "Teetotaler" who rarely if ever drank at all, fell victim to having "one too many." Missing Guard duty is a serious offense, AWOL, dereliction of duty, busted down in rank; any and all charges could be brought against that individual.

Being the Sgt. of the guard and missing his duty was even more serious.

The "Old man" Major Johnson (Not his real name) read Sgt. Studway the riot act on Saturday morning upon learning of the incident. Knowing that he was "short, very short" (Going Home) and that the good Sgt. was an excellent soldier, plus the fact a career was being planned, the Major showed some compassion . . . or so he thought. Sgt. Studway was ordered to be the Sgt. of the guard on the next night January 13th, since the Major believed the man now standing before him was still feeling the effects of the previous night, guard duty tonight was not an option.

Roy just arrived in Nam January 21, 1968-TeT.

Directed or ordered to pull said duty on Sunday night and then go straight to the "Freedom bird" that would take Dewitt home, back into the world.

As it so happened that Sunday January 13th, I was off, no guard duty for me tonight! To make things even sweeter, I was in possession of a small transistor radio and the Super Bowl would be on, not only that, but the N.Y. Jets (Yes, NEW YORK!) was playing against the Baltimore Colts for all the marbles. There is a twelve hour difference between Nam and the states, so at roughly 1:AM I'm laying in my bed inside of the hooch (Living Quarters) with radio in hand, eyes closed and envisioning the game. ERRING, ERRING, shrieked the base siren, it was a sound so high pitched and loud that it would make the hair on the back of my neck raise straight up. KABOOM, BAM, BANG, RAT-A-TAT-TAT, RAT-A-TAT, flares suddenly lighting up the sky, bright as possibly can. All of us scrambled from our hooch, M-16 in one hand and a bandolier containing magazines with ammo in the other. A few guys ran directly to the flight line and others jumped in a three quarter vehicle and drove to the ensuing attack. Enemy sappers had some how managed to slip past the guard bunkers, put explosive satchel charges on as many aircraft as they were able to, and then started to blow them up.

Mayhem was now upon us all, soldiers scrambled about, "Charlie" shooting at us, behind us and beside us. Unless one has faced what could be their own mortality, they can only guess what it may seem like. In the midst of all of this hell, it slowly and emphatically became clear to me that I was not going to survive this night. I'm going to die. Fear grips you unlike anything you have ever known. Ringing inside of your ears so high that it makes Church bells pale in comparison, the stomach tightens and your derriere starts to pucker. Something else also happens, adrenalin and . . . ANGER! As scared as you may be in that thinking you will die, you are equally as angry that the finality of life is now at hand. The combination of both almost seems like an oxymoron, yet strange as it is, with all that was happening around, I have never, ever been more focused.

IT WAS THE LONGEST NIGHT OF MY LIFE!

I do not need to close my eyes to remember, it is as clear and vivid today as it was then, many years ago. The raging gun fire slowly ebbed and then finally fell silent, the sunrise was just beginning to climb over the tree line to my left, exhausted and relieved, I silently thanked God.

A few of us formed up and started to sweep the area in a straight line, we walked with our backs to what was left on the flight line towards the perimeter. The area was littered with enemy dead. One dead sapper lay on his side with his left arm resting upon his forehead and his left leg bent at the knee, as if he was sunning himself by a pool. I was amazed to see that in his final earthly position, all the holes he had throughout his entire body and the glint of sunlight pouring through those holes. I remember this well. Another V.C. lay dead at my feet as I continued on, he was fully intact, except that his cranium was wide open and the inside of what remained of his head shined brightly, almost as if it had been polished. Towards my right, approximately three feet away, lay the dead sappers brain, fully intact as if it were removed by a surgeon, that is until I picked up a large rock and then dropped it onto the brain, causing it to shatter in many pieces. "Screw you," I silently said to myself and again continued on.

Remains of the two Chinook Helicopters after the attack,
January 13, 1969.

Now by this time dead bodies were removed and being removed both ours and enemy alike. Myself, and another soldier slowly came upon the command bunker, the same one I had been in so many nights before. Every one was dead, all six soldiers. The bodies had been removed shortly prior to our arrival and taken to a makeshift morgue that had hastily been set up.

It was reported that during the night of January 13th, the enemy sappers, who had knowledge of who and what was where, fired rockets into that bunker killing all who were inside of them. Dazed, confused from firing coming out from our own bunkers, many a life was lost; Sgt. Dewitt Studway was one of them.

IT WAS THE SHORTEST NIGHT OF HIS LIFE.

Sadly, he was to leave Vietnam and return home in just a few short hours to his family and loved ones. Inside of the bunker our boots sucked for air as we waded in the deep blue black blood that was thick and sticky, the flies and stench of death was among us; the price of war. A piece of human skull was imbedded into the wooden beam which was supporting the heavy sandbags that was the top part of the bunker. My friend Rich said that we have to bury this, and with that, slowly raised his hand and with a kind of reverence, removed the remains. Outside of the bunker I dug a small hole in the ground with my hands and together we buried it, it was an act we did in silence.

I have often thought of Dewitt Studway over these many years, a life lost like so many others, a future never realized, love nurtured no more, only memories. If then only memories remain, know this: There once was a man named Dewitt Studway, a kind and gentle man, a man who loved his family, a man who loved his country, a man who died too young. I remember, I will always remember.

My friend may your body rest in peace and may your soul rest in God's loving hands. Thank you for the opportunity to have known you and oh yes, thanks for that advice, long ago.

Your Friend and Brother,

Roy

TEDDY BEAR

People leave things at THE WALL: medals, old jungle boots, books of poetry, notes, toys, a teddy bear . . . . a tattered teddy bear. I pictured a boy's mother reaching into a closet where thing had gone untouched for years. I saw her open a box. Perhaps she didn't want to remember what was in that box, but she opened it. She saw the teddy bear and fell upon it, holding it tightly as she held her son.

The bear was her baby's companion. He toddled around with it, hugged it, held it by its arm, and carried it to bed. It kept away the monsters of the night. Every day he would tell her what he and the bear had done. And when she rocked him to sleep, holding this bear, he fought sleep, eyes closing slowly, as he would later fight death.

The bear waited a long time in that hour with nothing to do-no one to protect. The mother found it and took it to her son. Not to a cemetery of strangers, but to THE WALL, the still peaceful place where her son is among friends. There again with his boy, the bear can rest. The monsters are gone. And more than anyone else, more even than the mother, the boy and his 58,000 friends understand.

This letter was left at the Vietnam Memorial Wall Washington DC
by an anonymous person.

Dewitt Studway, Jr

Specialist Five
271ST ASHC, 307TH AVN BN, 164TH AVN GROUP, 1ST AVIATION BDE, USARV
Army of the United States
Durant, Mississippi
June 07, 1947 to January 13, 1969
DEWITT STUDWAY Jr **is on the Wall at** Panel 35W Line 085
See the full profile **for Dewitt Studway**

Dewitt Studway Jr
Specialist Five

PERSONAL DATA

Home of Record:	Durant, MS
Date of Birth:	06/07/1947

MILITARY DATA

Service:	Army of the United States
Grade at loss:	E5
Rank:	Specialist Five
ID No:	53669641
MOS:	67V20: Observation/Scout Helicopter Repairer
Length Service:	02
Unit:	271ST ASHC, 307TH AVN BN, 164TH AVN GROUP, 1ST AVIATION BDE, USARV

CASUALTY DATA

Start Tour:	02/01/1968
Incident Date:	01/13/1969
Casualty Date:	01/13/1969
Age at Loss:	21
Location:	Phong Dinh Province, South Vietnam
Remains:	Body recovered
Casualty Type:	Hostile, died outright
Casualty Reason:	Ground casualty
Casualty Detail:	Other explosive device

Comments from the first story, The longest night The Shortest Night;

- Ed Frank on Mar 20, 2011
  The years have distanced us from the Vietnam War but the special bonds we shared during that time will always be with us. A great tribute to a fallen buddy.
  A Fellow Vietnam Vet!

- Lennorelo on Mar 23, 2011
  A heartfelt story of a friendhip that not only saved a life but also a lost soul alone for the first time.

- Shirley on Apr 1, 2011
  It's a beautiful story about a caring friendship and it touched my heart.

- Carlos Fidalgo on Apr 6, 2011
  A wonderful story. Thank you. These stories and people cannot be forgotten. That bond of brotherhood will always continue for our veterans.

- Anna on Apr 6, 2011
  Thanks for sharing such a lovely and genuine story.

- Guest on Apr 6, 2011
  A beautiful story. Wonderful.

- Guest on Apr 6, 2011
  This story was very touching. Thank you for sharing it with us.

The people who fought so hard to defend their country will always be honored and their stories will forever live in our hearts.

- Megan on Apr 6, 2011
  This story really touched my heart. Thank you for sharing it with us. All those people who fought so much to defend this country will always be in my heart.

- Joe on Apr 7, 2011
  an amazing story.

- sean on Apr 7, 2011
  Great story that shows how precious life is and how war can take that away

- NS on Apr 7, 2011
  A beautiful and powerful story of two young soldiers. When you get the opportunity, thank a Veteran.

- Denisse C on Apr 14, 2011
  This story is very touching. I'm glad people can come out and share the stories with everyone. You're our true heros so thank you for all you have done for us.

- Rebecca T on Apr 14, 2011
  I felt that the story was touching, it showed the compassion that someone can have by just reading a story. I thank the person for writing this story because it shows how one thing can truely impact someones life no matter how big or small. The memory of this war and specfically this one person and this

particualr memory is something extrodinary that people need to read and realize that there are people out there just like them experiencing things that no one should have to experience in the first place. R.I.P Sgt. DeWitt your misse by the friend who wrote this story in your honer. Thank you for serving in this terrible war.

- Soubhana A on Apr 14, 2011
  This story really depicts the harsh realities of war and I truly thank you for writing about this . . . I appreciate all that you have done and the stories you have told about the war. Thank You.

- April on Apr 14, 2011
  This was a really sad story and makes me so grateful for all of the people that served in the Vietnam war and the soldiers who are in battle today.

- Gene Sullivan on Apr 14, 2011
  What a waste of a good man

- Chris B on Apr 14, 2011
  Thank you for sharing this story, I know it must be very hard for you. God Bless DeWitt Studway.

- Jon S—6 on Apr 11, 2011
  I felt bad when I read about after the battle was over and all the dead people. Most people never have to go through anything like that, and the people who did, need to be appreciated for there sacrafice.

- Cody F—6 on Apr 11, 2011
  I see that he had a lot of bravery and luck to survive this war. It shows how sad war is when his friend died in the last hours before going home. This story makes me appreciate what these men have done for our country.

- Anna V—6 on Apr 11, 2011
  When reading The Longest Night The Shortest Night, you get a sense of friendship and brotherhood. People who barley knows each other fight for one another's lives everyday, never looking back.
  I'm thankful knowing that I don't have to go through nearly as much as these soldiers did.

- Naveen K—8 on Apr 11, 2011
  Firstly, putting young souls out into the battle field is just terrifying. At this age, when they have just been given the title of adults we give them so much responsibility, such as Roy. This story tells us about how unpredictible war can be and how easily it affects many lives.

- Jesse G—8 on Apr 11, 2011
  This story was really eye-opening for me. It really described the soldier Roy's story very well and it kind of made you feel like you experienced it with him. You really have to have a lot of respect for Roy and all soldiers who risk their lives for our country. Unfortunately, this story ended up in the loss of DeWitt's life. This tribute really puts war in prospective because it showed the loss of life as well as the great relationships formed during it.

- Chyna W—6 on Apr 11, 2011

  I found this article interesting yet sad at the same time. How he was so happy at the thought of coming back to his wife and child and planning out what he'll do when he gets back.

- Afrim H—6 on Apr 11, 2011

  Silence or joy never last too long on the battlefield. I'm glad that a story was able to be shared so that the many who did not appreciate what they did would come to their senses. I just hope I never will have to go through such a thing.

- Matt G—8 on Apr 11, 2011

  After reading the letter that Roy had written, I, personally became even more knowledgeable of what war is really like. People today and even back then who have not served in out military do not understand what these brave heroic men go through each and every day that they are on the battle field. War is real, very real, and lives are lost, and if effects not only the men who are fighting around him, it affects the family members and friends of the person who died fighting for our country. Roy said it was the shortest night of his life. Reading this letter really got my attention and showed me how war isn't a fun thing. Dewitt's wife and daughter were now never going to see their husband or daddy and that is just so sad to hear. I, having family myself who serve in our military, know that feeling of "are they safe, I cant wait to see them, how long till they come home" that feeling doesn't go away ever, im sure that Dewitt's and Roy's and everyone who served not only in Vietnam, but every war America has fought in, have family who are always think about that them. In closing, I am very glad to have had the opportunity to meet and hear the stories of these men, not only are they interesting to hear, but that are eye-opening and have impacted my life greatly. And for that, I thank all the veterans and soldiers who fought and died for our country.

* Alanna M—6 on Apr 11, 2011
When I was first handed this story The Longest Night The Shortest Night in class I was like oh great now I'm going to cry like a little girl. But when I sat down and started to read the story I have to be honest I kind of giggled at the beginning. I never imagined that during war that people would make friends and look after each other so quickly. Also, while I was reading I felt like I was in the war with him because of the way he described the night his friend DeWitt was killed. I felt for DeWitt and his family because this good guy DeWitt was killed the night before he was to go home to his family. By the end of the story I had tears in my eyes.

* Alan T—1 on Apr 11, 2011
The war in Vietnam has a lot of significance to me and my family. My dad has told me about how much damage it caused—many times. He lived in Vietnam before coming to the US. When he was 16, he was drafted into the military service. He had seen the horrible outcomes of the battles that took place, and firmly resolved not to go. I just can't imagine that if my dad was just a little hesitant in his decision to leave Vietnam, I might be living in Vietnam today—without a father, or I might have never been born at all. Even though my dad described Vietnam so vividly, I could never truly comprehend the level of destruction that he described. Knowing stories from both sides of the battlefield,

it really makes no sense that these innocent people are forced to fight for the beliefs of their leaders. All (or at least, most) of the soldiers on both sides did not want to fight people in this way. If they met on the streets somewhere, one would not feel a burning desire to kill the other. It is really very sad that these good people are forced to fight each other, not knowing what the other party is really like.

- Crystal O—I on Apr 11, 2011
  I thought this was very informative and gave me a different prospective on what they went through in war. I think that everyone has their own views and ideas on what war may be like weather it's from video game interpretations or through a textbook. However, no one truly gets the actual feel and understanding of what war is like until they have the chance to hear about it from someone who has been there. I thought that it was inspiring how the veterans were able to comfortably talk about their personal experiences and their feelings. They were honest when saying their reasons for going to war and how they were treated coming home. The presentation was very informative and interesting. The personal stories left at the war in addition to the ones they had in the museum portion were very touching and expressed so much feelings that both the victims' families had and fellow veterans that went back. I personally found that the presentation was very inspiring and gave everyone a new prospective on the Vietnam war.

- Marykate O on Apr 11, 2011
  Thank you. Very nice, touching story. Thank you for coming to school also and educating us on this important event in history.

It was truly eye opening. You and all of our troops that served in this war and every other, are brave heroes. Thank you for representing the United States well. you helped me realize more about the danger of war and the courageous young men and women that fight in war. I wish you and your family the best.(you deserve it) I wish and hope that you\'re friend will rest in peace forever.

- Dana C on Apr 11, 2011
  This was an amazing, heart wrenching story. It put me in a whole new perspective of the war, I felt like I was there. It shows the bravery and courage these men held and the difficulty they had to undergo. Also thank you for the presentations at our school, it was a very emotional but eye opening experience.

- Matt F on Apr 11, 2011
  This was a very sad story. God Bless all of the soldiers and veterans. RIP Dewitt Studway.

- Anny r on Apr 11, 2011
  This is an amazing story. thanks for our school. It was a plessure to have you. we learned alot from the stories and also the pictures thanks

- Jessica M on Apr 12, 2011
  This story made me realize how much soliders went threw. Im sorry for the lost of your friend and all the other lives you have lost.

- Mary on Apr 12, 2011

  Thank you for sharing your experience with us. I am so thankful we have men and women like you willing to risk their lives to protect our freedoms.

- Melani Salibian on Apr 13, 2011

  Such a sad story! Its amazing to hear this from an insiders view. Truly tragic.

- Hansl on Apr 13, 2011

  sorry for your loss. thanks for coming in to share your experience.

- Steve Bergen on Apr 15, 2011

  I am touched deeply by this story and thank my friend Gene Sullivan for bringing it to my attention.
  Steve Bergen 4/15/11

- Allison on Apr 15, 2011

  Thank you for sharing your story with us. It shows how much courage you and all of the other soldiers fighting in the war had and still have. This has really opened my eyes to what actually happened during the Vietnam War. Thank you for everything you did for our country!

- JOHN P on Apr 20, 2011

  Great job Roy. A very touching tribute to a fellow Viet Nam Vet.

- Andrea on Apr 20, 2011
  Thank you for sharing this very moving experience with us.

- Dawn on Apr 20, 2011
  Although many of us will never truly understand the devastating effects war leaves on a person, your story has given us a glimpse into the eyes of a young men & women fighting for our country every day. We owe all of our veterans a "thank you" for their bravery and courage.

- marcus on Apr 22, 2011
  Like many other combat Vietnam Veterans, we all have stroies of Vietnam and how it has changed our lives forever; and like many other Vietnam Vet's we don't talk or write about our experiences, although we should. Unlike most Vet's Roy has taken the initiative and made the tremendous effort, to capture his experiences and write very well, of his fallen Brother Dewiitt Studway, it was a moving story that'll impact anyone who reads it. Thank Roy

- Laurie n. on Apr 23, 2011
  Very touching story.

- Linda on Apr 23, 2011
  Thank you for sharing this experience with us. It gives all of us a keen insight to your feelings under such horrible circumstances. It\'s nice to see the compassion you have for others. Thanks for all you\'ve done.

- Pat M on Apr 24, 2011
  Thank you all so much for coming in to share your experiences with us. It must be hard to unearth all of the memories and i really appreciate all you've done.

- Liz N on Apr 24, 2011
  Roy, thank you for sharing the story and the precious memories of DeWitt Studway. Very moving.

- Nick on Apr 24, 2011
  Sad story, goes to show the realities of war. Thank you for coming to our school and sharing everything you had to offer.

- Lois on Apr 24, 2011
  We as a nation are able to enjoy the freedom we have thanks to our brave men and women who serve our country. We should never forget them or the sacrifices they have made.

- Jonathan on Apr 27, 2011
  It\'s a sad story it shows the truth about war

- Connor McLaughlin on Apr 27, 2011
  Tragic story. Amazing how the vets could speak about their memories and shows their courage.

- allen goldberg on Apr 27, 2011
  Real life is sometimes makes a more powerful statement that the best fiction

- yo on Apr 27, 2011

  wow, really touching . . . stories like these open our minds in a way we could never imagine. Bravo.

- John D'Allara on Apr 27, 2011

  This story is very touching Roy, thank you for sharing it. I am very sorry for your loss. I appreciate what you did for this country. I feel it is hard to show the gratitude i have for you and all those who serve, the least i could say is thank you. THANK YOU ROY AND EVERYONE WHO HAS SERVED AND/OR IS SERVING IN THE MILITARY. OUR HEARTS GO OUT TO YOU. GOD BLESS YOU AND GOD BLESS AMERICA.

- Andrew Tschudy on Apr 27, 2011

  Great story, thanks to all vets for their sacrifice

- Pam on Apr 28, 2011

  We are privileged to be able to hear/read these first hand accounts from our Vietnam Vets. This is how history comes alive for those who are to young to remember it. It is an important part of American history!

- Paul Corriel on Apr 29, 2011

  very human, very real

- Theresa on Apr 13, 2011

  This story is very moving and exposes the reality of war. I appreciate the brave soldiers who risk their lives to ensure safety among us.

- Shane V on Apr 13, 2011

  Tragic story. Amazing how the vets could speak about their memories and shows their courage.

- Dan G on Apr 13, 2011

  after reading The Longest Night The Shortest Night I felt very bad for all war veterans. its very sad that they had to fight in war. But the story also shows how strong of a bond the veterans develop; living and dieing together

- James C on Apr 13, 2011

  This story is really touching and nothing I say can compare to what they have been through. It is a beautiful story. Thank you to Roy for writing and publishing it. All the Veterans I have met show so much courage and bravery whether on the battle field, sharing their stories, or both. God bless all our Veterans and active soldiers.

- Hannah M on Apr 13, 2011

  This story opened my eyes to what really happened in Vietnam. Not just facts, but personal accounts. I appreciate the vets telling us their stories, and I know that it can be hard sometimes. This story shows the dangers of war, and how everyone loses in a war. Thanks Roy and the other vets that tell us their war stories. RIP DeWitt.

- Danny G on Apr 13, 2011

  this was a great and touching story. i would like the thank all who have served and are serving. you have all risked your lives for the greater good of this country. THANKS AGAIN you deserve it!

- Shelby S. on Apr 13, 2011

  This really touched me, and made me realize how much more precious something is when it's gone. Thank you so much for having the strength and the courage to write this. I could never compare any of my own experiences with what I have just read. Truly heart breaking.

- Sarah S on Apr 13, 2011

  verr touching story, you are very brave to share your experiences with us, thank you for protecting us without you who knows where we would be now.

- Brendan M on Apr 13, 2011

  Great story. I can only imagine the pain these families went through after the deaths of these brave people. R.I.P. to all the lives lost in war.

- Erica D on Apr 13, 2011

  This story was both sad and eye-opening and made me thankful for all of those who served in the war then and serve in the war currently.

- Denisse C on Apr 14, 2011

  This story is very touching. I'm glad people can come out and share the stories with everyone. You're our true heros so thank you for all you have done for us.

- Rebecca T on Apr 14, 2011

  I felt that the story was touching. It showed the compassion that someone can have by just reading a story. I thank the person for writing this story because it shows how one thing can truely impact someones life no matter how big or small. The memory of this war and specfically this one person and this particualr memory is something extrodinary that people need to read and realize that there are people out there just like them experiencing things that no one should have to experience in the first place. R.I.P Sgt. DeWitt your misse by the friend who wrote this story in your honer. Thank you for serving in this terrible war.

- Soubhana A on Apr 14, 2011
  This story really depicts the harsh realities of war and I truly thank you for writing about this ... I appreciate all that you have done and the stories you have told about the war. Thank You.

- April on Apr 14, 2011
  This was a really sad story and makes me so grateful for all of the people that served in the Vietnam war and the soldiers who are in battle today.

- Gene Sullivan on Apr 14, 2011
  What a waste of a good man

- Chris B on Apr 14, 2011
  Thank you for sharing this story, I know it must be very hard for you. God Bless DeWitt Studway.

- Angela psy on Apr 7, 2011
  Thank you for sharing your stories with us. You are all really brave

- Morgan psy on Apr 7, 2011
  These are amazing stories that are truly touching. Thank you for enlightening us with these stories that will be hard to forget.

•Kiara on Apr 7, 2011
  I don't think i could have done waht you did back then. i cried as i read this pictured everything you went threw as if i went threw it myself.

- Caitlin D. on Apr 7, 2011
  Amazing story, thankyou for what you have done for us. By coming to our school and presenting stories like this it makes us have a better appreciation for what we have and more respect for people like you.

- Bruce McClintock on Apr 7, 2011
  About Vietnam . . . . I wish all the people who remember it could forget it, and all the people who forgot it would remember it.

- Jessica 6 on Apr 7, 2011
  It's hard to believe that these men, at such a young age had to face life and death situations like war. Many men had families and loved ones that they left behind, and some were never able to return to. Watching friends die next to you was more then I can imagine. Living with experiences like war, changes you and you're your outlook on life and it's hard for things to ever be the same again.

- mike psy on Apr 7, 2011
  very touching story, its upsetting how quickly 2 men can become friends in such a short amount of time, then comes to an end just as quickly. you are a brave man

- Justin on Apr 8, 2011
  This is truly an amazing and inspiring story. My grandfather was in Vietnam, I never really got the chance to ask him about it, considering that he died shortly after he came back, but I'm sure he had many stories like this as well.

- Collin on Apr 8, 2011
  Thank you so much for risking your lives in war for us.

- Sara on Apr 8, 2011
  It's crazy how these men went through so much at such a young age. They're been through and seen so much that some people didn't even realize. Sacrificing there life and leaving there families to fight for us all. These men are brave facing life and death situations that flash right before there eyes. Your visit to our school has opened a lot of our eyes to what you all went through, you are all very strong, the stories were touching and have helped us better visualized and have a clearer perspective of the Vietnam war. Thank you for sharing your stories and experiences.

- Samantha B.—8 on Apr 11, 2011
  This wirting conveys the pains of war how people loose friends and family in the bloody fighting and once they are gone they can't come back. This is a great tribute to his friend .

- Bethany G—8 on Apr 11, 2011

  I would like to begin my reflection by saying "thank you" to the person who wrote this.

  It was tragic (and you could really feel the loss) that the friend died so close to being able to go home.

  There are a couple of morals to this story.

  1. NOBODY wins in war . . . DeWitt had won, he was going home and he still died. Part or all of everyone their died.

  2. Friendship is valuable and sometimes you don't know just how valuable until its gone . . . he didn't know that his friend was going to die. He probably would have said more to him during that last encounter.

- Liam R—8 on Apr 11, 2011

  This story is a very sad and disheartening. Studway was a very young and capable man and to die at such a young age at the time he did is tragic. The fact that he was almost going home after a year of being in Vietnam is very upsetting. Also he was a father and a husband, his death effected many people and left friends and family brokenhearted. The condition that Roy had to see him is also makes this a very sad, and depressing war story.

- Sam K—8 on Apr 11, 2011

  I feel this story was sad especially since it actually happened makes this story even sadder. Its unfortunate that young adults of age 18 had to go to war and basiccally were forced to fight and kill others. Every day that these people were in war, guarentee they were waiting for that one day when they could finally go home and see there family. This really makes me feel sympathy for all slodiers past and present.

- Joe D—8 on Apr 11, 2011

  This story was a depressing story because Dewitt Studway was on his last night on duty and he was killed. It is upsetting if he died anytime, but to happen when he was one night away from returning home a strong healthy man. Also it was upsetting his good friend Roy had to see his friend in the condition he is dead when he knows his friend was going home

The Three Soldiers

BROTHERS

The thirteen month long tour in Vietnam can best be described as the most defining time of my life. All of the views, values and principles that I held were both changing and evolving. As a youngster, I was subservient to others in my thoughts and feelings.

Upon being honorably discharged from the U.S. Army, I found myself thrust back into a world that was alien to me. So much had changed for me, from the people, places and emotions, combined with little to no guidance from anyone. This made for a difficult adjustment back into "THE WORLD."

Although I may have physically returned to the world, emotionally I was still back into the Nam with "my brothers." Not until the last of them returned home safe could I feel some sense of peace. My thoughts would often drift back to them. I was always concerned for them because of the bond that had been built between us. I was fortunate in the fact that I was not sent to Vietnam as a replacement soldier. Instead, my buddies and myself arrived "in country" as a unit, the 271st Aviation Company.

This company was formed approximately two years prior to embarking to Vietnam. During that time, friendships were forged and strengthened and a bonding had begun. Young men, who work together, eat together, sleep and play together become as one. We were a family and we looked after each other just the same as any other blood brother would. The names of my brothers are still etched in my memory as if I spoke with them yesterday . . .

Roy outside of our
hooch in CanTho

Roy and his buddy-
M-16 rifle

A few of the guy's enroute to
perimeter guard duty

Ray Kral from Manhattan, New York, was our resident music professor. Rich Radowick from Michigan (a man so handsome that a Vietnamese hooker paid HIM for sex!). Gene Kramer from Long Beach, California. Bob Frost from Tampa, Florida. Carl C. Dennhardt from Oregon. Jimmy (JIMBO) Quinn from Michigan. Donald Hinote from Florida. Dewitt Studway from Mississippi. George Bell from Washington State. Last, but not the least, John Keller from California, who always made sure to brush his teeth SEVEN TIMES a day!

We shared the same living quarters, food and music. Music proved to be a great connection for the guys and I. In fact, a few of the guy's took an R&R (rest and recuperation) to Hongkong, and returned with reel to reel tape decks. Cantho Base Camp soon became home to The Doors, Jim Hendrix, Joplin (Janice, sorry Scott) and The Beatles. We had our very own concerts on the other side of the world. It was a nice form of escapism, a link to the far off world we remembered.

Approximately six months into our tour of duty, a replacement troop arrived to the 271st company. The N.F.G (New Fucking Guy) waltzed in, dropping his gear atop his rack and announced to no one in particular, "Hey Guys, Tom Chica here," with a half wave of his hand. As per usual with any N.F.G., he was greeted with indifference. Maybe a quick nod of the head, but certainly not a THANK GOD YOU ARE HERE! The guys and I quickly noticed that Chica pushed a little too hard from the beginning to enter our tight knit group. Instead of being quiet and easing in with all of us, he became overbearing. Not to mention his stark resemblance to Fred Flintstone was enough to keep him at arm's length.

One particular evening, I found myself all alone in our shared hooch and decided to take advantage of this rare quiet time and catch up on some letter writing to friends and family. Out of the corner of my eye I spot someone approaching towards me. It was none other than Chica. He was dressed in an Oriental silk, pajama jacket. In Chica's chubby arms, he was carrying a large BONG. It seemed to me almost comical that I was in the presence of Fred Flintstone trying to emulate Hugh Hefner. "Hey, where is everyone tonight?" Chica asked scanning around the hooch. "Don't know," was my reply without looking up. "Hey man, want to share my pipe?" This time I did look up. I made eye contact with Chica, I said in a clear and slow manner "I don't smoke. I don't smoke anything." Then I put my head back down and continued with my letter writing.

Now I readily admit that I am NO angel or even a boy scout. The fact of the matter was, I always wanted a clear head. For me, that was not an option. I don't even drink alcohol, but then again that's just me. With that said, I didn't judge any of the guys for their activities and didn't like to be judged for my disinterest in those activities. Plus, if I were ever to toke some weed; it certainly would not be in the company of that asshole!

Since I performed perimeter guard duty five nights per week, it was a day or so before I was able to sit down with a few of the guys after the Chica/Bong incident. When I bumped into Gene Kramer, a close friend of mine, he informed me of what had transpired the night before. Flintstone Chica approached several of the fella's hanging out in the sleeping quarters and opined that I was not to be trusted; by not sharing Chica's pipe I had committed an overt act in his eyes. Half smiling and slowly shaking my head, I inquired to Kramer what the response was. "We kicked his ass !!" was Kramer's quick retort. Who was that fat bastard to attack one of our brothers? Gene went on to say to me that he thinks it will be quite some time before Chica says anything about anything again!

Chica's luck didn't get any better. Chica was trained to be a door gunner on helicopters, a job in which he took great pain to inform all that he did not like. Of course, word spread and the Warrant Officers assigned to piloting the choppers along with the crew chiefs did not want him assigned to their ship. So Chica was reassigned to ferrying the pilots to and from the flight line via jeep, a pretty good gig. Along with his new job, Chica was informed that he now would have to perform perimeter guard duty on the bunker systems outlying the base camp.

Audie Murphy, Chica was not! He secretly (on purpose) let a few men know that his next plan was to shoot himself "accidently" in the foot while on guard duty. In his mind, he reasoned this would be his ticket back home. Soon thereafter we learned, to our surprise, that Chica did indeed carry through on his plan and shot himself in his foot! What was not surprising to learn was that this sharpshooter, missed! We learned that he pressed his M-16 rifle down so snug to the toe end of his boot that the round actually went BETWEEN his toes! This caused no more damage than a hang nail. Chica was such a fuck up, for cryin' out loud, it's almost darn near impossible to miss a target when the rifle is placed directly on top of an object.

Oh Chica, Chica, Chica. He would often like to brag that he was a New Yorker on his upbringing. But the guy's who were from the city would quickly and loudly refute his claim" was the retort. Chica, you come from Long island, don't think for a second "The Island" is New York! No way, No how. The thought of any association with this guy was abhorrent, he was not allowed to stake claim to the big apple. Now that Chica's plan A and plan B had failed, it was on to plan C or should I say, plan D ... DESERTION.

Being the mental midget that all of us came to know him as, his new plan was to take his R&R (rest and recuperation) to Hawaii, and then change into civilian clothes and purchase a plane ticket to his home. That was the last time any of us ever saw Chica again. His plan, the last plan was finally carried out. Goodbye and good riddance. None of us cared. Chica never became one of us, not then, not ever.

A month or so after, Jimbo Quinn, our very own Radar O'Reilly greets a few of us with a great big grin on his face. "Boy's" he exclaims, "Guess what I have in my little, old hands?" Before any of us could respond, Jimbo held up an envelope addressed to the Company Commander. It was a letter from none other than ... CHICA!

We unanimously agreed to open and read the contents, after all we reasoned, why should the C.O. have all the fun. In his own handwriting, Chica explains to the C.O. that life in Nam was too stressful and "blah, blah, waa, waa." He ended the letter stating that he would turn himself into the authorities. If it is promised that he will not be sent back to Vietnam.

We elected our most accomplished letter writer among us to draft a letter in response. Chica was directed to report A.S.A.P (As Soon As Possible) by "our newly elected C.O." to the nearest M.P Military Police). By failing to do so, he would most assuredly FACE A FIRING SQUAD, and unlike him, THEY WON'T MISS!!!

We never heard from Chica again, I assume wherever he is, he now speaks French Canadian. The rest of us went about our duty and completed our journey, HONORABLY, all my brothers and I.

Roy Tschudy

*Chica's name has been changed

Roy just finished up Bunker Detail

Just out of Basic Training Fort Jackson, South Carolina

UH-OH

I never gave it a thought as to how I would react upon my return to "THE WORLD" after Nam.

Joining the army at seventeen years of age with my mother's grudging consent; I was soon to discover that this was not a Boy Scout camp.

Basic training was designed to strip down a new recruits sense of self and then rebuild him with the ideology of us, we team. It was my good fortune that "Uncle Sam" could seem to care less about a recruits prior to civilian status, what job title was held or how much money a person had earned.

If you could run, crawl, do push-ups, properly maintain and use a rifle, make a tight bed with hospital corners, (thanks mom!) and be in excellent physical shape, the D.I. (Drill Instructor) would stay off of your case.

Now I was not blessed with brains or beauty, but what the good Lord did provide me with was the physical ability to not only meet but exceed at any and all training requirements presented to me.

The highest a recruit can score on the physical training test was a 500, I did a 490.

Only one fella scored a 500 on that test and I would have also, in my haste in the parallel ladder reaching the end to return I over extended and dropped to the ground.

That slip up cost me a perfect score, I was tied with two others for a second place, good enough to keep the instructor happy. A few new recruits would shake and quake in their shiny new boots when a D.I would throw a tantrum, for any sort of noncompliance. It never happened to me because I made sure not to give them a reason to do so.

Add in the fact that I was raised by a single Mom in the Bornx N.Y.; I learned early in life what real screaming was! Basic was held at FT. Jackson in South Carolina, three days of orientation followed by a zero week (a training week that was not counted) and then eight weeks of intense training. The toughest part for me was trying to figure out what the hell the D.I's were saying.

All of them came from the south and with a heavy, heavy drawl. Heehaw y'all him skedaddle now bout sheit! I didn't understand a freaking word, so I started to pull out a bush and pray that was what the Johnny Reb wanted. In fact, none of the guys from New York understand those rebels, our country was involved in Vietnam and these dudes were still fighting the Civil war for cryin' out loud.

They would try and taunt us with remarks as to how many people did we stab and shoot; I know y'all is gangstas up in N.Y.C ... And you don't know what a tree is.

I once replied to one of those taunts, "You know why Jesus Christ wasn't born in the south?"

I would again state the answer before a reply could be made, "Because GOD COULDN'T FIND THREE WISE MEN AND A VIRGIN!"

After that statement I was gold to my New York brothers. Soon after, an unspoken truce between us was realized and we did our best to get along for the rest of our training. Modesty was just a word without any meaning, if a recruit happened to be shy he learned quickly about his new surroundings in the army. We showered together, crapped together without any stalls, just a long line of shitters. Count yourself "lucky" if toilet paper miraculously was present, otherwise one was left to his own survival skills.

Our one D.I. was an Asian man from Hawaii; he was small in strature but large in mouth.

He would often threaten us with karate chops, we believed him, because after all, what the hell did we know. An orator he was not, to this very day I can still hear him order the troops, GIMME TWENTY, YOU MUDDA BUCKERS!

Never picked on me though, like I said before, my savings grace was in the physical realm.

Still, the most defining year of my life lay before me, I would be forever changed, both good and bad, and at times . . . very bad.

I served for thirteen months in Cantho Vietnam with the 271st Aviation Company; I did a month extension to receive an "early out" that was offered to anyone coming back from Nam with five months or less.

I was coming home baby!

I was coming home alright, but coming to what?

Intrusive thoughts were constantly my companion now, torn about now leaving my buddies, my brothers whom I was so close with, and coupled with the realization of finding employment presented a whole new challenge for me.

With a limited education and having no special skills aside from what the army gave me, I was a little concerned about where my life's journey would lead me. After all and try as I might, alas, there were no employment ads in the newspaper for perimeter guard duty, UH-OH.

Now back home adjusting to my new, old way of life was proving to be difficult for me. Sure, some things looked the same, but looking and perceiving are two separate matters.

The friends whom I had grown up with and shared so many childhood experiences, now seemed different. Not any fault of theirs, another path was traveled and our lives were now different, I was different. Funny, I now somehow had this unexplainable desire, need, to learn.

Like a thirst on a hot summer day, I could not quench that need, reading and absorbing books of all sort, politics, and world events, articles on subjects pro and con along with watching the evening news became a compulsion for me.

Taking Webster's Dictionary and introducing a new word per day so that I could expand upon my vocabulary became the norm. Watching the evening news was difficult because the war in Vietnam was still raging on and my buddies were still a part of it.

I was home physically, but mentally and emotionally I was still in Nam.

I stayed that way until all of my brothers were back home, or so I thought.

The news cast could begin, "today, two hundred Viet Cong were killed in the Mekong Delta in a major offensive the U.S., we ONLY LOST x amount."

Anger and frustration would rise in me as I would scream back at the television, Asshole! How dare you. The insensitivity of the media elite made me want to puke; the loss of one American was one too much.

For that soldier, sailor, marine, air force member, all is over, no more hopes. No more dreams, no chance to be a Dad, no more hugs, no more kisses, nothing . . . no more.

Now multiply that . . . "ONLY" . . . by his Mom and Dad, sister and brother, aunts and uncles, cousins, nieces and nephews, friends and all who knew this hero, life now changed.

But not to worry my friends because, after all, he was . . . "ONLY."

Shame on them, shame, shame.

How does one realize when he slowly sinks into a state of mind where fuck you, fuck everyone, have taken hold of your life? It was a descent into an abyss where I did not care much about anything or anyone. Anger was my issue, not drugs or alcohol.

I now felt that "I had the right" to argue with anyone, and if a confrontation was in order, well so be it.

I foolishly thought that even if I get my ass kicked, I could at least break the other guy's nose.

I also remember two incidents I was involved with on my return from Nam. Sadly, it is and will always be painful to me, an argument with my younger sister about who knows what led her to say in anger, "I wish you were still back in Vietnam."

She never had chance. My hands were tightly wrapped around her throat in a split second, filled with anger.

My poor Mom began smacking me with her frying pan yelling for me to stop.

Smack, smack, smack, the harder the smack the harder my squeeze became, either God intervened or the frying pan she used took its toll, I released my grip and silently walked away. Although my sister and I are close today, if I never apologized for my actions, I humbly do so now.

I am sorry Lenore.

The other incident that I can reflect upon soon after my return home had to do with a brand spanking new car just purchased by moi.

Sitting at a red light on Boston Post Road in the Bronx, the vehicle in front of me rolled back and into my front fender as the traffic light now turned to green.

Nothing.

I did nothing, I ate it and continued on my way, not happy mind you but not nuts either.

Not yet anyway

A few blocks down the road another red light was upon me, as I slowed to a stop guess who was in front of me? None other than Mr. Fender Bender. I made sure and gave extra room between us, the light turns green Bingo!

Instant replay!

Shmucko then drives off like nothing has happened, no excuse me, no I'm sorry, no is there any damage.

He drives off, that's it.

At the next red light, I jumped out of my car and banged my fist against the driver side window, he was somewhere in his mid to early forties and weighed near 210 pounds. I uttered two words to him, and they were not "Merry Christmas," the window rolled down about four inches and he returned the same holiday greeting. Four inches was all I needed, my hand reached through that opening and I grabbed hold of his thick black greasy hair face meet Mr. window, Mr. window meet Mr. face, and again and again and again. Horns were honking, traffic was backed up to Canada in both directions, now satisfied with my reinstruction on driving 101, I calmly walked back to my car and went on my way. Anger and crazy is a bad combination, I was both.

During the next forty or so years after Vietnam, I have been guilty many times regarding anger management.

Thankfully as a member of Vietnam Veterans of America Chapter #333, joining this group of fellow veterans has been an exceptionally wonderful experience for me.

I was not alone, I am not alone, but together in special group meetings and with the Veterans administration, we slowly begin to understand the word ...Why?

God is good, I have been given more than I deserve, and I am morally committed to help others, especially those who have served.

Members of V.V.A. Chapter 333
left to right: John, Jay, Roy, Andrea, Brian, Bruce and Marcus
Not shown: Gene S., John M., Yitz

Roy and wife Lois, June 2011 in Hawaii

June 2011 Pearl Harbor

ON THE JOB

I was assigned to the New York City Transit Division with the New York City Police Department for a shade over twenty three years.

Every police officer throughout the U.S.A is aware of the dangers "the job" presents, the flip side is the many other experiences we as police officers also encounter. All of us have had patrol shifts that are mundane and maybe even a little boring, but being an N.Y.P.D officer, I must confess are few and far between.

During my years "on the job," I ran the gamut in every aspect of police work, from every day interactions with the general public combined with the machinations and pressure the department places on officers.

Countless books and television shows/movies have cast the police officer in both good and bad plots showing the attraction and negative attraction of being a police officer. The only people in my humble opinion, who know and understand these features are police officers and to some extent, spouses of men and women in blue.

The general public goes about the daily work that is their job, they perform and witness basically the same routine the work allows.

Police on the other hand witness things that most folks would find abhorrent we get to witness the belly of the beast.

Very few instances are black or white, with police work a whole lot of gray area is present and each brings with it a separate set of circumstance.

The training of a N.Y.C. police officer is second to none, and it is that very training when applied correctly will determine the outcome of incidents that officer was involved in. There is no other job that I am aware of that is second guessed as much as a police officer, from the media to the public to city hall and the department itself.

A few bad apples in the department can and usually does, create a sense that all officers are corrupt and adhere to their own agenda, many times a P.O. is in a damned if I do, damned if I don't position.

Most officers do a magnificent job performance risking life and limb to do so, keep in mind that when the shit hits the fan, most people run AWAY but the officer runs TOWARD the problem, it takes a special person to do this job.

The different experiences encountered by officers at times fall into stories that would make it into RIPLEY'S BELIEVE IT OR NOT! Mostly it would be in the "NOT" believable part of the story, here now is a few of my own experiences as a police officer in the city, hopefully there is a statute of limits and the department can't slap me!

It was a beautiful clear July summer morning when my partner Kenny Mack and I drove off in R.M.P. 111 (Radio motor patrol is a police car) starting off our tour of duty for the day. The two of us were riding in a large suburban type vehicle carrying with it an assortment of all type equipment for emergency purposes.

We were on patrol for all of one minute when radio dispatch notified us of a subway street grating collapse at 116st and

Lexington Avenue located in New York's Spanish Harlem. Arriving on the scene we both observed a large deep black hole on the street sidewalk where the subway grating cover was halfway collapsed into the hole creating an accident prone condition.

I immediately relayed the severity of this incident to dispatch and requested that the N.Y. Transit Authority be notified and to send a repair crew ASAP.

Kenny was already placing large orange comes around the four corners of the opening and attaching bright yellow police tape that read, "POLICE DO NOT ENTER" to each end of those cones.

Sgt. Steve Tresca soon arrived and after making his own observance of the condition directed Kenny and me to remain on the scene to ensure the safety of the public.

Remember to keep in mind, this is N.Y.C where the curious seekers of the entire world reside and just because a hole the size of the Grand Canyon appears out of nowhere with large orange cones and bright yellow police tape attached to them will then deter people from performing their own investigation.

As the day wore on more and more folks were gathering around the crater before them and offer up each one's hypothesis with question on top of question.

"What happened officer?" Also, "Anybody fall into the hole?"

One rocket scientist at the scene declared that this was the work of a meteor from the sky.

Being told since my childhood that I possessed an unusual sense of humor that has now followed me to adulthood, there are situations that present themselves just begging to be addressed.

God help me, but I cannot resist the urge to help pull a prank and coupled with my partner Kenny Mack who lives and breathes for the same thing, makes for a fun event. So, here is the scenario the two of us have, one VERY large ground opening that is VERY deep and VERY dark, combined with a VERY large and VERY curious crowd of people, two police officers with VERY good imaginations all which equals up to a VERY interesting story. Kenny bends down under the yellow police tape with his large black mag flashlight in hand and shined it into the large dark hole slowly and side to side.

With a studious look on his face and a beam from the light continuously moving back and forth, He blurts out loudly "I see it! I just saw it Roy!

Hurry and get the Rope get the rope!!!" I swear to the almighty that I'm trying not to laugh and somehow nobody noticed that I did, directing my speech to Mack that the rope is not long enough and I will have to call it in to headquarters.

As I reached for the vehicle radio microphone I asked my partner loudly If It Is what we think it is and should I make sure that headquarters notifies the zoo?, "Yeah, call it in now before this thing tries to escape!"

If you thought these onlookers were curious before, now hearing that . . . IT was somewhere in the deep dark hole before them and that the zoo was notified, now created all sort of speculation.

Kenny turns to the throng of people gathered and states it is important to stay back and not make any loud noise or quick movements, we don't want . . . IT, to get angry.

Tell us what it is, we got to know man, Kenny said "O.K, but beware, it's a . . . RANDOZZ!!!!"

Awhatozzi? No man he said a RONZONNI, Yo bro, them things are mean I seen them suckas on channel thirteen (13) for those animal shows.

What do they look like officer?

My partner Kenny Mack was now in his glory, for cryin out loud the Pope from the Vatican balcony could not have had the attention of the masses more than what Mack had now before him.

Mack explained, "A RANDOZZI is a cross between a HYENA with DOZZI spots on its head and neck area and a TAZMANIAN DEVIL RAT."

How big it is? Ken went on to say that "IT" weighed about Forty pounds and was three to four feet long depending on if it was a male or a female.

If the RANDOZZI feels threatened he will rock back on its tail and cross his eyes, hissing and growling then he will leap at the throat of the closest person to him and try to claw and fang them.

"Just stay back folks" Mack directed the crowd; we need to keep the RANDOZZI calm. During this time I'm wondering when the hell the Transit Authority is going to get here and fix this damn grating.

We could send a man to the moon and back before these guys get here. Just like the game of telephone, our three foot RANDOZZI has now taken on the lore of a ten foot man-eating lizard that lives deep in the subway system and used to live in the zoo.

By now it is the afternoon and the crowd of neighborhood people has swelled to try and get a glimpse of a RONZONNI, Mack was conducting the crowd better than Leonard Bernstein at the philharmonic when I notice the Duty Captain arrive on the scene in his vehicle. Snapping out a sharp salute and greeting him with a "Hello Cap, things here are under control."

The question raised by him was about the size of the crowd just for a broken subway grating? I did my best that I could muster and stated to the Captain that Kenny and I were just giving an explanation to the crowd for the need to be aware of accident prone conditions and the steps to avoid them. I also said this is a good community relation idea to keep people informed on being aware.

"Outstanding!" Keep up the good work officer, signed my memo book which indicates his presence and then as quickly as he arrived also departed the scene.

Freakin' Kenny did not even notice that the Duty Captain came and left, he then decides to take this whole charade to the next level. Putting on heavy work gloves and grabbing the dog pole that is used to restrain vicious dogs, Kenny states loudly for all to hear "We can't wait any longer, I'm going in!"

People actually yell to him that he should wait for the Y.M.C.A., I guess people sometimes can be confused between the "Y" and the ASPCA, and after all its letters are just the same.

Some who were peering over the police tape now swore that they indeed saw the Randozzi even pointing in the direction the elusive critter was running to and from.

Bro, that thing is smoking fast, it's like lighting! Man, that thing should run in the Olympics, crazy fast.

Not only had Mack convinced some people that a Randozzi existed, he now had some folks convinced that they actually can SEE the critter; a better bullshit artist would be hard pressed to find.

A third platoon (3:30pm through 12:00midnight) relief RMP now arrived on the scene to relieve my partner and myself for the rest of the day, Mack now decides to break the news to the crowd of RANDOZZI watchers that indeed no RANDOZZI existed. It was just a joke made in good fun. It was just a subway grating accident, that's all it is.

The response was, "You ain't foolin us, we seen that RHAPSODOLLI and we are waiting for it to get caught! You can leave, but we know it's down there."

The two of us stepped into the suburban for the ride back to our command when Officer Rich Corry approached my window, quizzically he asked why was there so many people standing around looking into the grating hole?

Looking Corry straight in the eye I replied "Beats me."

Kenny Mack slipped the vehicle into gear and off we went, just another day at the office.

Roy-"on the job"

EXCUSES
FOR A SUMMONS

I think it is fair to say that people do not like to be on the receiving end of a summons issued by a police officer.

Some respondents grudgingly accept the ticket and say nothing to the officer writing the document while others have an excuse at the ready.

The offender at times will try to minimize the infraction committed while comparing it to some crime of a greater nature, such as why did you stop me when all of those other cars were also speeding? And, why don't you get the drug dealers and murderers instead of picking on me?

The standard reply that I would always give to the whiner was while glancing at my watch, "Gee it's ten after one; I catch the drug dealers and murderers at one twenty so I only have ten more minutes to issue you this summons."

With a smile, and wishing to have a good day to the operator of the vehicle coupled with a warning to drive safely, an unhappy camper slowly drives off.

I believe most officers are more than fair on decision making on the issuance of a summons, when an overt act is committed that person will be appropriately dealt with, either a summons or an arrest to follow.

However, many times when an infraction witnessed by the officer has occurred and the driver is not only respectful but states he acknowledges that the error was his and his alone, the wiggle room that officer has, may lead to just a warn and admonish as the penalty.

One of my fondest memories of denial was that of a well dressed gentleman who had recently been the recipient of a summons from an officer in the command at where I was assigned.

This man literally came into the command waiving a summons in the air and in a voice one level below Pavarotti declared to the desk officer, "I deny the allegations and demand to see the alligator!"

One time observing a young man complete an Olympic high jump over the subway turnstiles and fail to pay his legal fare, he was apprehended by the Captains team. Asked by myself for the reason that he failed to pay said fare; the youngest said that he running late for his class at the local community college.

As required all police officers must do a quick background check on an offender to see if he/she is eligible for a summons, when asked if he was recidivist (Repeat offender) the student shook his head side to side and emphatically stated "NO, I'm a Sagittarius."

Other answers came in the form of, my mother is dying at the hospital, and I don't care if you are the police, you work for me because I pay your taxes!

There were times that just to keep the day interesting, Kenny and I would ask a person in a temporary custody if they would like to participate in the Mayor's I.Q test provided to the police.

For whatever reason, most offenders gladly accepted the challenge to show that they were equal to the test questions.

Since Kenny and I made up these questions and they were willing to participate, we agreed that any answer given to us would be CORRECT.

Q. Who was buried in Grants Tomb?

A. The tut dude

Q. What city is East of West Chicago?

A. Mexico

Q. Finish the sentence: The grass is greener . . .

A. When you water it

Q. A bird in hand is worth . . .

A. Depends on what kind of bird

Q. You can lead a horse to water but . . .

A. He has to be thirsty

Q. Which is larger, three feet or one yard?

A. Three is always bigger than one

Q. If you drop a bag of ten pound feathers and a ten pound bag bricks from a building roof at the same time, which one will hit the ground first?

A. The bricks! The feathers be floating down

Working in the South Bronx also meant interacting with more than a few people of different ethnicities and cultures.

Diversity could be separated from block to block and would behoove any police officer who happened to work in these areas to be aware and sensitive to people. What may seem natural to one community may well be insulting to another, all in all people are just people good and bad just like everything else.

While interacting in these communities both my partners over the years, Kenny Mack and Rich Corry came across some very unusual names of people, in fact they were so different we had to double check many times.

The list, I kid you not, were: Rufus Swampfox . . . Cleotis Golightly . . . and my favorite name of all . . . Festus Notoes.

Sometime we had a hard time explaining to Captain Richards that these were all legit names and that we were not making them up on a summons.

On patrol one time, Mack and I came on the scene of an injured lady who had slipped and fallen down, an aided report was prepared and the name given to me was Femal'e Ortiz. Never knowing of a name of that sort before, I inquired on how it came to be that she had been named so unusually.

Her mother was an immigrant from Santo Domingo and spoke very little to no English at the time of her birth. When it came time for the nurse to fill out the required forms, her mother was asked what the new baby was to be named.

Not comprehending what the nurse was asking, her mother just smiled and shrugged her shoulders, the nurse then filled out the hospital part of that form and where it asked for the newborns name, Ortiz, Female was inscribed.

The new mother believed the hospital named her new child, named her femal'e.

Just because a police officer is assigned a lunch hour does not necessarily mean that he will receive that lunch time.

After just purchasing hero sandwiches and finding a quiet place to park and enjoy our meal period, a large bright blue Cadillac roars directly past our clearly marked N.Y.P.D vehicle, without stopping at the corner STOP sign.

Lunch no more, lights and sirens on; the caddy is brought to a fast halt. Approaching the vehicle from both sides, the vehicle operator complies to put his keys on top of the roof of the car. Mack asked the driver for the required I.D license, registration and insurance card.

The driver is a middle aged man of color who when speaks has a distinct Jamaican accent, he is polite and cooperative.

"Roy," Mack calls to me, "check this out" while looking at the license of the driver. The license revealed a photo of a Hispanic man in his twenties and the name Juan Morales assigned to the document. "Whose license is this?" I asked this gentleman, the reply was, "Don't blame me: It's the police's fault."

Further explaining that the week prior to this he became involved with a minor fender bender with another car, a police officer came over to both drivers and asked if either one of the drivers was injured.

Both drivers said to the officer that they were not injured and then the police officer "Told us to exchange licenses," so we did.

Kenny Mack and I returned all of the documents to this vehicle operator and said to him, "Have a nice day."

...We still managed to eat the sandwiches.

PERVS

A veteran police officer, who worked in the same squad as me, had one time worked in the department's robbery unit.

As officers must often do, an exchange of events that have taken place during his tenure are discussed among us, locker room chatter. This can be an informative time and a learning experience as well, when you think that you know all that there is about police work, it's time to get out and retire.

I inquired of him the reason why he opted out of that unit after spending three years collaring up bad guys. Jim was a big strapping Irishman with a large gray moustache and a brogue to his voice that sounded almost musical to the ears.

He said that many times over, both he and his partner would be assigned to different men's bathrooms in the N.Y.C. subway system, many robberies occurred inside of them when the victim was standing at a urinal, a decided disadvantage.

Inside of the bathroom area there are small cubicles, pipe chambers consisting of assorted plumbing fixtures and an assortment of pipes.

Inserting themselves into the pipe chamber the two undercover officers now out of view would lay in wait for a robbery to be committed.

The downside to this Jim would go on to explain was that the smell in the bathrooms were so obnoxious that he wanted to puke after everyday. Beside the stink there was another aspect that turned his stomach on a daily basis and that was the gathering of the perverts and acts committed. Jim said that in his opinion if another fella wants to love another fella, that's their business, but when they take it to a public place then it is unacceptable.

Describing a few incidents observed.

At 86thst. Street and Lexington Avenue on the uptown subway side, one and sometimes twice a week a man dressed professionally would enter into a commode stall, he would then remove a jar of Skippy peanut butter from his attaché case and spread the contents thereof around the rim of the toilet and when finished, sank to his knees and licked the toilet completely clean!

When his mission was accomplished, the toilet licker would slowly and calmly place the jar of peanut butter back inside of the attaché case and exit the bathroom just as if this was as natural to drinking a glass of water.

"I used to love peanut butter and jelly sandwiches" Jim exclaimed," Now anytime I see a jar of Skippy I want to barf!"

"Not to mention that smell I can't get rid of, I could work for the rest of my life in a flower shop and I would still smell shit!"

I could not take it anymore was the explanation given, and knowing of my own encounters with pervs I understood.

A few of the other neat little tricks that these pervs would do is actually make a hole in the stall divider and then give a blow job to the other perv in the attached stall with his shwantz protruding through the perv made hole.

Very innovative were these cretins, when I was a uniformed patrolman and as part of my patrol procedure would do a bathroom inspection I always was prepared to find something out of the ordinary, always!

I would literally kick the entry door open as hard as possible to make sure that if someone was on guard duty looking out for little old me he would be the awardee of a fat lip or some contusion of any sort.

Entering the den of ass fuckers, I would make a fast observance of the entire inside of the room, generally speaking as soon as any police officer would enter a men's bathroom it would clear out faster than you could say, lunch is over!

Looking down to the bottom of a shitter stall it appears that some gentleman who just completed a shopping trip to Macy's with his Macy's bag tucked safely beside his feet, must have a bad case of the shits because of the grunting emanating from inside the stall.

I observe only two feet solidly planted to the floor but by virtue of instinct and experience, me thinks that something is not kosher.

Once again, the stall door is kicked in by me and lo and behold what do you think was in the shopping bag? Or rather, who do you think was the Macy surprise? None other than Mr. and Mr. pervert themselves!

Mr. perv #1 sitting on the toilet and his partner perv #2 standing inside the Macy's bag receiving a flute cleaning.

There is no way do I want or need a collar (Arrest) of this sort, I direct these two low life's to hit the road and find a room instead, these creeps buckle up without saying a word and just vanish into thin air.

Good riddance!

Eventually the Transit Authority wised up and closed all public bathrooms throughout the entire subway system, with crime rising, this was one way to curtail it.

Some life style these people live, and to think that at one time in each of their lives some mother held and rocked her little baby boy to sleep only to have him grow up to be a shitter eater, it could be worse . . . well, I guess not.

KENNY CHULDIE—WOMEN AND NO BRAINS

Certain members in the police department stand out as characters in their own way; one of these men in blue was another squad partner of mine for a short while.

Kenny Chuldie was a veteran officer and a very good one at that, street smart and book smart who later in his career rose to the rank of Lieutenant.

Kenny possessed a set of balls as large as the city we worked in, and in addition to these qualities Kenny claimed so be the world/s greatest lover with tons of ladies. Any attractive female that came across his path would be subjected to the charms of this Don Juan, hello beautiful, are you married?

If the answer was affirmative, a follow up question was ever present, well, do you fool around? This guy was undeterred and could not be embarrassed in any way at all, women are like flowers he would say, "They are here for me to pick."

Kenny would strike quicker than a cobra when it came to women; I use the word cobra because Kenny would make any snake proud.

Lover boy took great pains to inform the guys that he was dating a hot stewardess and whenever she was in town for a lay over it meant that "HE" was the LAYOVER!

One night we were paired up as partners for the first platoon, (Midnight tour) it was late spring and the night was misty.

Chuldie informs me that his stewardess girlfriend is in town and we were going to drop by for a quick visit.

So what if we are going so far out of sector that a moon landing would be closer. Kenny was obsessed in his quest to visit the angel of the skies. All I could think was thankfully we were in an unmarked police car so that the chance of being observed out of sector was greatly reduced, and admittedly I was anxious to see this babe we all have heard so much about.

"Wait in the car and monitor the radio" was directed to me as Kenny parked directly in front of her apartment in lower Manhattan.

Crap, I really wanted to see this hunk of draws and hoped she had a roommate that I could meet.

Surprise, surprise, in less than fifteen minutes Don Juan is back inside the RMP, explaining that she was very tired after a long flight and she needed to catch up on some much needed sleep.

Just as we started to pull may from the curb the apartment doors of the building suddenly swung open and out came the "hot" stewardess remembering to give Kenny information about a flight plan of some kind.

My jaw, now dropped, mouth agape as I looked at this flight goddess, Kenny Chuldie did indeed have a really hot stewardess for a girlfriend that is if she was a stewardess with Orville and Wilbur Wright at Kitty Hawke, "Are you shitin' me Chuls? How freakin' old is that broad? She must be the only stewardess with an AARP card I continued, I thought that they had to retire from the job, not die on it.

"Screw you" was all the great one could muster to me as we headed back to sector. As soon as we were back to where we were supposed to be, I told Kenny that I was going to phone into the command to make sure that nothing untoward happened in our area while visiting Miss America ... 1906.

"Hey Brian" I say over the phone to the assistant deck officer Brian Barret, "Anything going on?"

"It's kind of quiet tonight." All's good Royboy, no problemo's, hope it stays that way," "Yeah me too, I'll check back with you a little later Bri," "10-4 Roy Boy."

As I was hanging up the phone an odd and strange feeling slowly set upon me. That feeling was from behind and up the middle of my legs. What the ...?

A hand was now on my testicles and gently squeezing (Thank God) and massaging my balls! Turning my head I see a very pretty lady of the night "in clear view to all, holding onto my nuts."

Before I could utter one single word out of my mouth, from the unmarked police car is my partner Kenny Chuldie with his head out of the window pointing and laughing, tears flowing from his eyes.

"My massager" who also has a huge grin on her face, nods to Chuldie's direction and says "He told me to do it," "Gee I would never have guessed, I replied." Chuldie was a character beyond compare, nothing or no one bothered him.

The uncanny ability to insult people no matter what race, religion, sex, height or weight and yet do so in such a humorous manner that rarely angered anyone, made working with him in the same squad interesting and fun.

Joking and kidding around in the locker room was common place, nothing and I do mean nothing was sacred, everything was considered fair game.

Winston Jones was an African American police officer with just as much time on the job as Chuldie. The two of them were always insulting each other much to the delight of any who would be in ear shot of listening to these verbal wars. Some guys actually would arrive for patrol a little earlier in the hope that the two of them would be in the middle of trading quips, it was hilarious.

Chuldie was slowly losing his hair, a serious blow to a man who was so very deeply in love with himself.

One Monday morning while bagging up for patrol, Chuldie comes strolling into the locker room with a brand new do, an afro!

All of us knew what would happen next and we were not at all disappointed. Winston arrived a few moments after Chuldie and when he laid eyes upon him with the new quaff, Winston hit the floor laughing with such a high pitched falsetto it sounded like a pack of girl scouts.

After ALMOST gaining his composure, what all of us were waiting to hear was now in full diss mode. "GODDAMN man, y'all look like one of them three stooges, or Bozo the clown with your hair all electrified like that" Jones said while holding his sides.

"You were always ugly Chuldie, but now you fugly!" "You may try to get a brothers fro, but you ain't never gonna get the size of a brothers dick!" Winston, in full attack now.

Looking at Chuldie you could see the wheels spinning inside of his head, finally replying, "Yeah, but I still have something that all brothers never had and never will." Surprisingly, Winston took the bait, "What's that?"

"Brains Jonesy, B-R-A-I-N-S" Chuldie stated as he slowly spelled each letter of the word, "Take a close look pal, because this is the first and last time you will ever see an afro connected to a head with brains."

The obligatory fuck you were exchanged between the two before the high five and slap on each other's back, both laughing exiting the locker room.

If some unsuspecting soul ever wandered into our locker room during these verbal battles. I bet they would think a war between the KU KLUX KLAN and the Black Panthers was taking place, in truth we were all the same color ... BLUE! As fate could only have it, the following week this dynamic verbal judo duo was partnered up for a day tour in the RMP covering a Manhattan sector.

Directed by the radio operator to respond to "a man under" which is a person who has fallen underneath a moving subway train at the 77th street subway station, Chuldie and Jones arrive on the scene quickly.

They learn from an eyewitness that a man walking between the subway cars of the north bound number six train when he suddenly disappeared. As per training, Officer Winston immediately requested power off; this is done to effectively stop the subway trains from moving.

When notified in return that all power to the third rail has been shut down, both Chuldie and Winston descend onto the subway tracks. As they slowly back track where the train has just came from, both officers walk gingerly, flashlights in hand searching for any sign of a human body.

Midway between the train stations they come across a large object lying near the third rail, upon closer inspection they find a man most definitely deceased.

Chuldie shined his light onto the face of this unfortunate soul and observed a heavy set African American man in his thirties with a gaping head wound.

"Jones" Chuldie states to his partner, "I was right! Take a look at this!"

Shining the beam of light on the body and slowly directing it toward the head, the head cavity revealed nothing but an empty cranium.

"See, I was right all along," Jones quizzically replies, "What?" "He doesn't have any brains; this is what I've been telling you for years!" "Fuck you Chuldie, fuck you!!!"

CAPTAIN SKIPPY

Captain Mark Richards, our commanding officer never saw a subway station sign that he didn't want to possess for his collection.

Countless times he would direct his two most trusted officers to add a screw driver with their handcuffs and weapons in case a subway sign became available.

Skippy, as my partner Kenny Mack and I always addressed him, was a human bloodhound with regard to smelling out a NO SMOKING or NO TRESPASS subway sign. Retrieving the booty for the Captain was not difficult for the two of us: for the most part the signs were going to be replaced with newer ones any way.

One assignment given to us was something akin to Treasure Island; we were given a map and told that at Grand Central station a certain subway sign, no longer being used could be relocated from the inner sanctums of the earth to the safety of Skippy's office.

Arriving at Grand Central we descend four levels beneath the subway station, both of us have our flashlights to help direct us and feeling like Indiana Jones in search of the Holy Grail, in our case . . . a subway sign.

Now, deep down inside of Grand Central station where we are closer to China than N.Y.C. in complete darkness and following the direction of the map. Turning a sharp corner the two of us come to a sudden halt.

Directly in front of us just as the map described, the valued treasure was right before our eyes, the blue enameled subway sign with white letters and boarder read: NO SPITTING! $25 Dollar Fine.

For God's sake, we were literally in the bowels of the earth where no human could have ever possibly ventured; I was surprised we didn't come across molten lava or a creature of unknown origin at the very least.

Removed with the precision of a Neurosurgeon with our trusted Phillips Head screwdriver, we returned triumphantly with the treasure, carefully wrapped in burlap cloth to ensure no damage to Skippy's acquisition.

Captain Richards was a huge train buff and loved everything associated with them. My guess is that he would rather Mack and I arrest a perp for graffiti to his beloved subway system as opposed to a murder, unless that is if the blood from that murder somehow stained a subway bench.

My partner Kenny Mack and I were two officers that comprised his team, the Captains team. We were responsible for an assortment of tasks that comprised of issuance of summonses, arrests, graffiti reports and truancy and during the summer months assigned to the N.Y. Yankees baseball detail.

To say that Kenny and I wore many hats is an understatement; our feeling was that there was nothing that we could not accomplish.

We both admittedly were at times a little too big for our britches and over stepped our boundaries more than we should have, nothing illegal just a little pompous.

Kenny and I were good partners together, very good in truth.

The similarities we shared was striking both of us born and raised in The Bronx, both Army Vietnam Veterans, both married with kids and the love of sports. We were so in tune with each other that a word not needed to be spoken between us, just a glance would suffice, and it became uncanny.

Since the both of us were mischievous, we took great delight in chop breaking, especially when it came to our leader Skippy Richards. Kenny and I knew the Cap's psyche very well and we knew when to have a plan ready if ever the need for one would arise.

There was a time when our entire command was facing renovations, piece by piece. As usual, the commanding officer was first in line for the job. Skippy's office was fairly large and contained his own bathroom, not a bad little perk to have.

Every morning like clockwork, just after the day tour fell out for patrol, Skippy with newspaper in one hand and pipe in the other would direct the desk officer to hold all calls while he closed the door to his kingdom and completed his constitutional.

With his office now in repair Skippy was relegated to use the crapper in our locker room, a bathroom that consisted of two urinals and two shitters, one of which was delegated for prisoner use with sign attached to the stall door.

Not one officer that I know of ever used the prisoner toilet for fear of who knows what crawled out or the ass of some miscreant.

As per Skippy's M.O. his daily routine was somewhat inconvenienced although unchanged. I often wondered if he ever took at dump at home or just saved it up.

Kenny and I were presented with an opportunity that was too good to resist, early one day we scoured the locker room for a pair of boots, finding some on top of a locker, the two of us quietly entered the men's locker room and placed the boots inside of the police officers commode stall and closed the door.

It now appeared if someone is inside the stall answering nature's call, boots expertly placed on each side of the commode. Within minutes of the 2nd Platoon day shift exiting the command for patrol. Skippy grabbed his newspaper and ever present tobacco pipe and headed straight back to the area where the toilets were located for his daily deposit.

Later that morning filled with curiosity, my partner Kenny Mack phones into the assistant desk officer and friend Brian Barret if anything interesting happened this morning in the command.

Barret informs Kenny that Captain Richards wants to see the both of us when we return to the command, explaining you guy's probably can guess why.

"What happened Bri?" It seems that the good old Captain went about his usual routine; he took newspaper in hand along with his tobacco pipe and went north to the toilet only to return shortly mumbling about something or other.

Five minutes later, Skippy repeated the quest to try and empty his bowels only to return in a highly agitated state.

By the third try to the crapper, Skippy was now beyond the point of no return, he marched back to the front desk with the smoke coming out of his pipe like it was a locomotive, he ordered officer Dubinski to enter the men's bathroom and find out which officer is in the toilet stall and to get him out ... NOW!

Less than two minutes pass when Dubinski returns to the desk officer area with a large black boot held chest high in each hand.

El Captain was now holding his newspaper so tight looked as if the print would be squeezed right off of the paper; Dubinski informs the Skipper that there was no one inside the toilet, only these two boots.

Thru gritted teeth Captain Mark Richards directs the desk officer "Find out where Tschudy and Mack are; tell them I want to see them both before the end of the day!"

With ass cheeks squeezes so tight that they could crack a walnut, Skippy waddled off toward the toilet area finally free for his constitutional.

Just before Kenny and I were to end our tour for the day and as directed, the two of us entered in the Skipper's office.

After eight hours, the Skip was calmed down even to the point of being mellow, "Hey Skip" I said knocking on his open door, "You wanted to see us?"

Sitting in his king size chair reading police memo directives he didn't even look up at us, slowly making head side to side he quietly said, "Don't you guy's ever stop?"

This seemed more like a plea than a question, Mack said in return, "We can only promise to try Skip, just don't make things so easy for us."

Any other officers would be doing patrol in Siberia by now, but Skippy generally liked each one of us and also knew that he could count on his two men squad to complete any job description presented, and we did it well.

Besides subway signs, Captain Richards other love, was to own vintage cars, not toy cars mind you, but the real deal.

And so it came to pass that one fine day, Skippy in all of his glory drove into work inside of a mint 1962 Oldsmobile convertible car, pipe in mouth and fedora hat on top of his head with a grin that any new papa would have.

The car was in such mint condition it looked as if the vehicle was hardly ever driven and that's because it hardly ever was.

I asked Skip after congratulating him on the purchase, where did he find this beauty and knowing him also well, did he get a good deal?

He said that a neighbor had recently passed away and his widow who was elderly and did not drive just kept the car inside of the garage. Skip proudly stated that he purchased the Vehicle for fewer than three thousand dollars a real steal.

No truer words were ever spoken.

Every few years the area where the command police officers park their own private vehicles is repainted to enhance the yellow lines for said parking.

For two days all of us scramble to park our cars where ever we can find a decent area to do so. The one place we all know NOT to park our vehicles is directly under the elevated train structure, nuts bolts, bottles anything and everything falls from the track area and with it almost certain damage to one's own car.

Of all people to make this boo-boo, the last person one would think to do so is The Captain. Our very own Skippy and yet that was just what he did.

If trouble is invited, then trouble will come.

Trouble this time took the form of N.Y.C pigeons perched up high underneath the elevated tracks directly above . . . you guessed it!

When Skippy ascended the street subway stairs he was met with the sight of his mint olds covered in pigeon shit, he nearly had a conniption.

Witnessing a grown man standing on a sidewalk corner looking up towards the heavens and pointing and shaking a clenched fist interspersed with dialog about death and pigeons, is a sight one won't soon forget.

The next day while out on patrol, my partner Kenny Mack suddenly pulls the vehicle off to a curb and excitedly exits the car. Wondering what he was up to, I also exit the vehicle only to observe Kenny bending over and scooping a dead pigeon into a large paper bag.

"Now what?" I inquire to my partner, knowing full well he was up to something. After placing the carcass safely inside of the bag, the trunk of the car was opened and Kenny retrieves a toe tag designated for a dead human body, under the details inscription Mack writes in "I confess to shitting on your car."

Toe tag properly affixed to the claw of the departed, we drove back to command. Arriving shortly thereafter, the two of us head straight for the Captains office with the D.O.A. firmly tucked under Mack's right arm.

Entering the command we both take note of Skips absence from his office, the remains of D.O.A. is now placed on top of Skippy's office desk, we slip out of the office as quietly when we entered into it.

The Skip later enters back into the command after attending a meeting with other command Captains as they are all directed to do on a monthly basis. Kenny Mack and I follow directly behind him as he walks into his now refurbished office, stopping and turning towards the two of us obviously in thought about the meeting he was a participant in.

"We want you to rest easy Skip" Mack states, "We got the bastard, it's over."

Reaching up and removing the glasses from his face, Skip with a quizzical look replied, "What are you talking about?"

Mack just points to the Captains desk, "Take a look." Skip takes his seat and opens the bag containing a dirty and dead stiff pigeon with a deathbed confession attached to the right large claw.

Continuing on, Mack goes on to say "That freakin' bird is done crappin' on your car Skip; He never had a chance with me and Tschudy on the case."

Captain Richards didn't know whether to laugh or cry or remove his 9mm glock and just shoot us, "Get out, get out now and take this crap with you!"

"O.K. Cap" we said almost in unison, taking the winged culprit with us and depositing the remains in the nearest garbage can, outside of the office.

Mack and I agreed to be good for a while and let things simmer down; we were wise enough to know that if you play with the bull long enough, eventually you'll get the horns!

GROWING UP IN "DA" BRONX

1951, my parents moved into Parkside Projects in "Da" Bronx, N.Y.C. This housing community was a brand spanking new sprawling complex, consisting of approximately twenty buildings. The folks who inhabited these new dwellings were mostly WW2 veterans and their families. The ethnicity make up was in the vicinity of 95% Irish, Italian, Jewish and also German heritage.

Our family moved into a fourteen story building, this being my Dad, Mom, older sister Holly, four years old, myself two years old, and Lennore, the youngest at one year of age. We lived on the ninth floor overlooking other smaller buildings where people lived and worked. Three short years later in 1954, my Dad suddenly and unexpectedly passed away in his sleep of a heart attack. He was just forty one years old. No pension, no social security, welfare assistance was never an option for Mom. She quickly gathered herself. She worked two jobs and learned secretarial skills by night attending school. In those days, neighbors would watch over one another and treated children as one of their own. Just one large extended family you might say. Today, they may call this child abandonment, but times were different back in the fifties. We were all cut from the same cloth. The Housing Authority was as polite and sensitive to Mom's plight as one would drink acid for water. They demanded that we vacate our two bedroom apartment and stated that we would be "permitted" to move to the Edenwald Projects, which even then was akin to a state penitentiary.

My Mom may have been born at night, but it surely wasn't THAT NIGHT! She was a tough Bronx lady, and she informed the H.A. that they could put the demand where the sun doesn't shine!!! A compromise was reached and we moved from the ninth floor, down to a one bedroom apartment on the seventh floor. I learned early in life not to mess upwith my Mom, because that 5'0, 90 pound lady could turn into a fire breathing, sledge hammering superwoman in a nano second, and anyone who dared hurt her kids would pay for it dearly.

We gradually settled in and went about growing up and experiencing life with all of its ebbs and flows. I had many friends as I grew up in 660 Arnow Avenue and many memories that I cherish to this very day. My best friend was Donald Mastracchio. Donald also lived in "my" building on the fourth floor. He lived with his Dad, Don, his Mom, Gene, and his younger brother Frankie. They sorta adopted me as one of their own and would always include me on trips and outings. I came to love them as if they were my own family. Other friends included Reese and Bruce Trubow, Gregory Tozzi who was the group comedian, Eddie Tobias who never wore sneakers as a kid, David Koslovski, the card player, the Charap brothers, Paul and Richard, and last but not the least, the oldest and nastiest, the toughest in our group, the bully, Teddy Tischler. This group of kids grew up together, knew each others families, slept over at one another's house, ate and went to church or synagogue together. Life was well in our little world, and our world consisted of about a three block radius at that time. Anything further seemed like taking a space shuttle.

We would gather together and play. Play anything and everything. The basketball courts were just across the street, it had four separate courts, and we practically lived there. As I stated before, Eddie Tobias only wore shoes and was forever landing on another one of the guys foot causing all kind of howling and screaming. I think every one of us experienced some sort of foot disfigurement because of Eddie's shoes. To this day I would doubt if Eddie owns a pair of sneakers, he probably owns a string of shoe stores! Donald was a pretty good athlete as a youngster, and would play anything suggested by any one of us. Another thing he loved was my Mom's potato pancakes and goulash. When Mom was cooking that meal we knew Donald would soon ring the bell. I also loved his Moms meatball and spaghetti dinners and would make myself available just as Donald did. We were pals.

During the summer months, we would be up and ready to play as soon as the sun would rise. One or two of us would start to gather the rest and "call for' the guys by ringing or knocking on the door of each one's aptartment. The Charap brothers, Paul and Richie had a few peculiar oddities that the rest of us always semi-enjoyed. We always needed enough men to field a team and this required all of us to be available.

Upon ringing the bell, Millie who was their mother, would open the door and greet us in her apron and bra! No disrespect, but Marilyn Monroe she was not. We would be allowed into the apartment to get the boys. A point of interest was pictures posted on the walls. I mean all of us had in our homes some kind of art or picture of something, but the Charaps took it to another level. They would cut out the Sunday color section of the Daily News and tape it on the wall, on the wall for cryin' out loud! Posted directly near the front door was the picture of 1959's Miss Rheingold beer, taped with both scotch and electrical tape mind you.

We'll be down after My Little Margie and I Love Lucy would be the same reply Monday thru Friday. The brothers talked about Margie and Lucy as if they were next door neighbors! Trying to get Paul and Richie to play was a task in itself. But we needed to have enough guys to field a team for the day. Gregory Tozzi was our neighborhood jokester and always had something ready to say. One time he teased Paul and Richie about they're middle names, which happened to be Preston and Murray.

A TV show in the 1950's was on Saturday's and it was Sgt. Preston of the Yukon and his dog, King. When they finally came down, Gregory would announce to one and all loudly, "Here comes Sgt. Preston and his dog MUARRY!" All of us would get a chuckle every time it happened, all of us except the brothers that is.

On rainy days David Koslovslti (don't call me Kos) would break out a few decks of cards and begin to teach the rest of us new card games. Dave always had a toothpick in his mouth like his Dad, Harry, we wondered if he slept with the dam thing. Dave knew all of the card games imaginable. At ten years old he could have been dealing blackjack in Vegas! Reese and his younger Bruce were always ready to play and had great parents, Warren and Doris.

On occasion, the boys would argue, but not anything like any other brothers would. Tough Teddy Tischler, Yep, that's what we called him (behind his back of course). He was the oldest of us, the one who cussed, and the loudest, biggest, meanest kid in our building. None of us particularly liked Teddy or liked playing with him. We thought he was a bully. As an athlete he was average to below average, not to brag, but I could run rings around him in any sport. To be fair, tough Teddy wasn't always mean and when he acted nice. It was a good time for the rest of us as well.

I recall, one time a group of us were heading over to P.S.96 for a softball game when tough Teddy stated in his best Al Capone voice "Lez go blay!" Koslovski falls down laughing, tears flowing and holding his side and mimicking tough Teddy. Lez go blay, Lez go blay. We have all since grown up and gone our separate ways. One time we even had a neighborhood reunion and many of us gathered for the first time in many years. We reminisced and spoke of the times we shared in our youth about growing up in "Da Bronx." We were fortunate to have had each other as friends as well as each other's family. It was a time of innocence, a time of bonding, a time that I will never forget, growing up in "Da BRONX!"

Roy Tschudy 9th floor, 7th floor, and the 4th floor, Whew!

Growing up in "Da" Bronx was not unlike growing up anywhere else in the U.S.A. in terms of language. For instance, in the South one who may be seeking directions will be greeted with an answer such as, "Over yonder or down the road a piece." For anyone not from that part of the woods they probably think to themselves, "Where the hell is yonder?" Down the road a piece may register a little easier to understand, but that "Yonder" thing is a whole different mystery to me. Then again, if a visitor from say, Alabama happened to find themselves in Brooklyn N.Y. and asking a resident thereof the same question for directions they may as well be confounded by the answer. "Fuggedabouutit" to anyone from the "Big Apple" means just that, for get about it.

In "Da" Bronx we take things to another level and have perfected the art of condensing a sentence into one single word. Why waste energy and suck up perfectly good oxygen to ask a question when a one word inquiry will suffice?

For example, "Jeet" is a word that although not found in Webster's dictionary and only because he was not from "Da" Bronx, is as common to Bronxites as "Yonder" is to a Southener. For those of you who are not familiar with New York linguistics this is the scenario for the word "Jeet." It is a beautiful summer's day in "Da" Bronx and it so happens to be twelve o'clock noon and I happen to run into my friend Johnny Palmero on Allerton Ave." Yo John house it goin?"

"Badda Bing" say's John in reply and then the famous Bronx word appears, I ask "Jeet?" and John nods affirmatively "Ham sandwich." See what I mean? Why waste all of the energy and clean fresh air to ask a question when as I stated before, one word would suffice.

In "Da" Bronx we even have our very own terminology regarding food and ordering it in a dell or pizza store. "Gimme a bagel and a shmear" is understood to be a bagel with cream cheese. "Two with Kraut and a square with mustard" are simply two hot dogs with sauerkraut and a potato knish with mustard either on top or inside of it. Let's say that you are hungry but not ravenous, so you enter a pizza parlor and you "Just wanna slice." Again, in New York one does not have to purchase a whole pizza pie, the pie is sliced into eight pieces and it can be ordered in any combination, ahh, the beauty of New York!

At fourteen years of age my friend Donald and I were invited to a house party across the street from our building 660 Arnow Ave. We were excited about the invite because we both knew that two hot babes were also going to the party.

Marlene was a very pretty girl with long light brown hair that swirled midway down between her shoulders and back, she always had a smile on her face and was as friendly as she was pretty. Then there was Rena, slender with short brown hair also pretty but a sexy kind of pretty.

The discussion between the guys's when it came up regarding the two girls was always about which one was hotter, it usually was a split decision. Either way, it was agreed that one could not go wrong choosing between them, pretty or sexy. Of course, here we were in an awkward growth surge as teenagers with not enough hair for a moustache and a voice somewhere between adulthood and Minnie mouse, no experience with girls and yet we have the onions to talk about them.

Donald and I first had to overcome a little hurdle with his parents and my mom, the party was to be held across the street in the Coops. This sprawling housing development was built in the nineteen thirties and actually was the abode up until WWII of the American Communist party members. After the war it was sold to a private enterprise with new families moving into the housing and the former moving out. None the less, this was the nineteen sixties and the cold war with Russia was in full bloom. The wall separating East and West Germany was philosophically speaking the same between 660 Arnow and the Coops.

To this very day if I close my eyes I can still hear my Mother warning me, "Stay away from the Coops, there's Commies in there!" Some how both Donald and I managed to persuade "The Patriots," so the party was a go.

That Saturday evening the two of us dressed up handsomely, enter into "The forbidden zone" and begin to ascend to the fourth floor where the party was held. I said to Donald, "I guess Communists also don't believe in elevators."

Music was playing and a large group of kid's was already present as we entered thru the apartment open door. When it came to dancing, at fourteen years old I was pretty much a spaz with the moves of some thing akin to a person having a Grand Mal seizure. Turning around from the tap on my shoulder I was confronted with pretty/sexy Rena, "Want to dance with me?" It was a slow dance song and although nervous I was equally excited for this opportunity.

Taking her hand into mine and pulling each other close, I felt a strange sensation come over me. I was being stabbed! The stabbing was coming from what ever was inside of her bra; I thought boobies were supposed to soft and bouncy. Those babies were like steel knives penetrating into my chest and the freakin song seemed like it was never going to end.

When the music ended I mumbled something like humma, humma, gonna get a coke or something as strange as that. In a flash Donald was at my side, "How was it? Was it good?" Still rubbing my wounds I assured my friend that it was great and now it was his turn.

After four or five records of the upbeat kind a slow dance song came on and Donald made his move. The look on his face half way into the record almost made me choke on my Frito Lay potato chip! Donald who I may add danced like Boris Karloff in "The Mummy" had a sort of shocked look in his eyes. Rena's boobs had struck again, she was a serial boob sticker!

We did not say anything about each one's stabbing until the next day, I asked Donald if he felt the same points into his chest that I had, after confirming what I already knew, it was agreed that sexy does not always win over pretty!

A SPECIAL FRIEND

Today I lost a friend, not just any friend, but my very own "Special Friend."

Before "Sam" joined our family, the four of us: Lois, Dawn, and Andrew, sat down and discussed the certain needs and responsibilities it would take from all, if indeed Sam was to join us.

Now the Tschudy family may not possess the largest house that surround the area, however, it is big enough for all of us to share with more love inside that the size of the Taj Mahal could not even compare.

From the very first moment that I met Sam I just knew in my heart that everything would be okay.

Dawn at eleven years of age and Andrew a few weeks shy of his eighth birthday took to Sam instantly and in the same fashion, he with the two of them also.

Although quiet at first, Sam was soon talking up a storm and everyone of us enjoyed our conversations with him. We soon discovered that Sam, who actually preferred being called Sammy, had some very peculiar characteristics, nothing bad mind you . . . but different to say the least.

For instance, his dining techniques were a wonder to observe. My wife Lois is a wonderful cook and makes a variety of different meals, she enjoys preparing these delectable dinners for all of us.

When she is preparing the meals in the kitchen Sammy would mousy on over and start one of his conversations continuing it right up until dinner was served. Lois generally served Sam first and I suppose that he felt honored because he literally dove into the food before him without uttering even a single sound.

Sam never complained about the wife's cooking, he ate everything placed before him except maybe string beans and it would be gone in a flash! Sam liked to putter around in the front yard a lot, always looking for someone to talk with.

Our neighbor, Eileen O'Neil was his favorite target and always would have her laughing with his continuous yakking. Yak, yak, yak, yak, yak! Oy Vay already.

An additional hobby of our new friend would often take part in was singing, especially if he heard me warbling out a tune, Sam would chime right in for a duet to the pleasure of no one.

Please take note that in the years of singing together there was not a single recording contract was ever offered to us, the world's loss I imagine ... well maybe not.

Sam loved to take family trips and visits, his favorite one was always when we piled into the car and drove to New Rochelle to greet Lois Dad, Grandpa George.

Grandpa was a widower and lived by himself, when it came time for all of us to get together for a day or so, Sam made sure to be included with the family.

Grandpa and Sam soon became fast buddies and really enjoyed each other's company, whether having a catch or just watching T.V. Grandpa always made sure to have Hagen Das ice cream available for the kids and Sam who always was ready for seconds.

Anything on television that had to do with animal shows' was Sam's favorite. If any show had dogs on it he would get excited and then would try to imitate them making doggy noises, even a howl or two.

On occasions that Sam would make up his very own self made songs, Gramps would laugh until the tears rolled down his cheeks. In fact the two of them got along so well that Grandpa would invite Sam to spend a weekend with him every now and then.

Of course we had to drive Sam down to Gramps place and make sure that he knew about the certain responsibilities in caring for Sam.

As the years passed, Sam easily became a part of us, a true member of the family. Yes, he did have his share of special needs which primarily were both his eating and toilet habits, but when you grow to love a gentle soul, a loving spirit, then there is no sacrifice . . . no sacrifice at all.

It has now been more than a dozen years since Sam came into our lives and so much has changed, Grandpa has left us and a hole in our hearts remain.

Dawn has grown from a seventh grader or a third grade teacher with many credits in hand, especially her husband Anthony who was her high school sweet heart.

Andrew has grown from a little boy to just graduating from college with a Bachelor of Arts degree, and through these passing years Lois still looks as young and pretty as a brand new bride.

Finally, I have long since retired from the police department after twenty three years on the job and now suddenly, without notice or warning, Sam has left us too.

So very special was Sam, so loving, so trusting, loved by all.

No more quiet evening walks . . .

No more songs to sing . . .

No more love to give or be given . . .

Only memories that will live in our hearts.

Thank you my friend, my very special friend, for when the gift of love is given it can never be forgotten.

You touched our lives with such love and happiness; we were blessed to have had you as a member of our family.

I take peace in knowing that God our father has brought you home.

So my special friend, until we meet again, thank you my sweet Sammy, thank you for being my dog, I love you.

Love, Daddy

Sammy

"Moya Duscha"

George Baranin

1915-2005

Moya Duscha George Baranin 1915-2005

Grandpa and Sammy

"MOYA DUSCHA"

He was 89, a month shy of his 90th year. Six foot tall with broad shoulders, still a strapping figure after all these years.

One could not look at "Grandpa" and not take notice of his legs.

Oh those legs, long and bowed at the knees, as if he spent years on the rodeo circuit busting broncs instead of a kid who grew up on the streets of the Bronx. His hands were akin to the size of a baseball glove; big and strong, yet gentle to the touch. George had many physical characteristics that made him unique in a funny kind of way, but then again nothing to laugh about.

Way before he became "Grandpa" or even "Dad," he was just George. George was born in the spring of 1915 to immigrant parents who arrived in the states just a few years earlier from Yugoslavia.

His father was named Mirko, or Michael in translation, like many others before him came from all different areas of the world to seek a new and better life for himself. After a short while in Mirko's new country, he became involved with other fellow Serbian folk and helped to build and establish the Serbian. All life and activities centered upon the church: social events, exchanging political views, everything and anything in life, the church was the center for more than worship.

She was just seventeen, alone, a little bit afraid yet determined to find her path in life. Her name was Mileva, but better known as Millie to her family and friends. She arrived knowing only her native tongue and nothing else. It was here in Manhattan in the little Serbian community that both Millie and Mirko crossed paths as it happens on an everyday basis from the beginning of time, the two fell in love and married.

From this union, two children were born and raised in the borough of New York, named the Bronx.

George was the first born to Mirko and Millie Baranin in what is now a long gone hospital of New York City. As the story has been recounted many times over, when the new born babe was presented to his mother, she cried out loud, "This is not my baby; you have given me the wrong child!" After the doctors and nurses conferred, sure enough a mistake had indeed been made and the proper "switch" was conducted. To think, if not for a mother's intuitive love and instinctive resolve then our Grandpa, our Dad, could have been named Miguel! George could have been the biggest and oddest looking Puerto Rican in the whole Bronx!

The long road of life for Grandpa had just begun and a collision was adverted right there at the inception. Who knows, maybe there was a reason why for so many years George would love to travel to New York City to watch the Puerto Rican Day Parade ... he always said it was so very colorful and the people are all so very happy and friendly, kinda makes you want to go, hmmm ...

A few short years after George was born, a baby sister arrived and completed the Baranin Family. Darinka, or "Dari," as she came to be called through her life was a dark haired beauty, who gratefully never inherited the same set of legs as bronco bustin' George.

Throughout the years that I came to know Grandpa George, he would reminisce about his early years and many aspects of his other years as well.

"Ten o'clock, Lights out!" This was a story that Grandpa would reflect upon every other visit at the Tschudy's. It seems that when Grandpa was a mere Lad and even until young adulthood, Mirko would shut the house Lights at ten pm sharp every night, no questions asked.

When my father said "lights out", he meant lights out, end of story. It seems that Grandpa was not like many senior citizens in that he would recount memories and repeat them many times over with the same enthusiasm as he had the first time around. Of course, the Tschudy's would react with the same "Oh, really, I never knew that" attitude each time Grandpa told one of his stories.

Moreover, Grandpa would add onto his stories, "as a matter of fact, I never had a birthday cake growing up." Now if that wasn't enough news to cheer you up, we were treated to the news that Christmas presents were but a mere dream to little George. Just when you figure you have hit rock bottom listening to these gut twisting, eye watering tales, Grandpa would chime in with, "you know what else, my father never said I love you to me." I use to think . . . gee thanks for sharing with us Gramps, I needed that like a hole in the head!

But you had to know Grandpa, for you to know him meant that you had to love him. Because whatever sad tale or story George would recount about the years spent with his parents, he always, and I mean always, unequivocally proclaimed his own deep love and admiration for both his mother and father. This was just a small part of who George was. A man who loved his family first and foremost, leaving every other thing in his life second. This was truly a great man.

George would share stories of shooting marbles on the sidewalks along with the other kids and playing stickball until all hours. The boys' would accept challenges from other neighboring kids regarding these games. To hear George tell it, one would think they were listening to a story about the "OK Corral."

Inevitably when Grandpa would join us for Sunday dinner and my bride, Lois "his daughter and heart beat," would make a fine spread with baked potatos. We would soon be informed with "you know, did I ever tell you that when I was a kid, me and the guys would sit around one of those old garbage cans. We would put bricks in 'em, paper, wood, and whatever we could find and start a little fire. It could be ten below, we didn't care at all, we would get a hold of some potatoes and roast 'em up. What a meal! We'd tell stories and my friends and we just really enjoyed each other's company." If I heard the potato story once, I heard it a thousand times. Funny, but I wish that I could hear it again, just one more time.

Speaking of eating dinner, this was an event that would always be talked about days and sometimes weeks after. Admittedly, it was mostly me who was doing the talking, but I also had Andrew as my sidekick. You see, when Grandpa joined us at the table it was like something out of medieval times! God love him, but the belching and excess flatulence was as normal to him as a duck to water. "Dad," Lois would sometimes chide, "please say excuse me when you belch at the table." This, of course, was meant to set good manners for our children, Dawn and Andrew. As well intentioned as Lois was, most of the reply received from Grandpa was, "What you never belch?" Score another one of the old timer. Of course when

Grandpa decided to join in conversation it would seem he always had a mouthful of food at the same time. Me being an army combat veteran was prepared for mortar attacks, but poor Andrew! It seems that he would always be bombarded with the peas or corn kernels. The poor kid was shell shocked! On the other hand, Dawn would half smile that I guess she wasn't under fire. "Dad, close your mouth when you're talking with food please," Lois begged once more. A plea is just a plea, and that plea lasted all of thirty seconds until the next fork full that is. Once again, I wouldn't mind another "attack" just one more time.

Additional stories included working at the railway express where "It was so cold, I had to stand inside the icebox to get warm." Can you imagine if Grandpa had any fish stories?!? Grandpa never flew in an airplane, "I'm not going up in one of those things for nothing," he would often say. "If God wanted me to fly, I would have wings!" Grandpa further recounted how during World War II in London he used to watch all those planes come flying in and then some of them crashed on the airfield. When it was explained to Grandpa that German anti-aircraft fire may have had something to do with that he replied, "I don't care, I still remember." So the closest that George ever came to flying was taking the elevator to the top of the empire state building.

In his day, George was a baseball player. Not just any ball player, he was the best pitcher in or about the area. He was so good, he was dubbed with the name "Monty" which is the same as the Ace, #1, Top Gun, The Big Kahuna . . . well you get the idea. Other than his family, which was his true love, nothing except baseball brought more passion and meaning to George's life. He signed a contract with the New York Giants, not too shabby! He was just that good!

However, love is greater than passion and as much as passion means at the moment, love lasts longer and runs deeper. In this case, love was in the form of a pretty, young sweetheart . . . Shirley. The first time George saw her in the candy store drinking a malt, he knew that was the girl for him and to whom he would marry. So George gave up his dream of a big league ballplayer and married the girl of his dreams. Make no mistake about it, if George wanted to pitch in the bigs he could have. As told to me in person by a gentleman named Vito Valtenetti, who himself pitched seven years for both the Chicago Cubs and White Sox, "He was better than all of us," claimed Vito. Vito came from the same neighborhood as George and knew well of the exploits of the well known "Monty."

After a few years of marriage, George and Shirley started a family of their own. A son was born to them, Richard was his given name and the passion was passed on with little to no effort. Father played and taught the game to a most loving son. They were inseparable, as if joined at the hip. They shared the same passion for baseball that George alone had in his youth. George was there for many, a game Richard pitched in, high school and college. Richard went on to pitch in a semi-pro league and George was present to root him on. Although Richard had the same passion as Grandpa, alas he did not share the same fast ball.

Richard's talent served him well in life and he went as far as he could ability wise. Like his Dad before him, Richard's passion ran deep and when his skills as a player left him as a winter's snowy field yields to the warmth of a fine spring day, Richard still carried his love/passion onward. If not a player, why not a coach? A dedicated and fine coach he became, leading groups of immigrant kids, not unlike his grandfather before him, onto fields of play in the midst of this there always was George. Home games, away games,

George was there for his only son, his boy. In this sense love and passion became intertwined in, the big man's life. Love for his son and passion for the game that meant so much to him ... more than my words can ever note.

Then there was, is, and always will be Lois. She was born to George and Shirley on December 5, 1955, eight years after Richard. Lois was a gift from God, no doubt. Many a tear and many a laugh were shared between the two, father and daughter. The term "bonds of love" falters when trying to describe the relationship of a pair of hearts as these.

My Lois would say many times over how fearless she was as a little one, often driving her dad a little bonkers. Whether it be a day of excursion out with the folks at a large outdoor pool, where Lois jumped off a diving board into, the deep end of the water without the remotest idea of how to swim or as a teenager putting make-up on using the downstairs mailbox as a mirror against her father's wishes. These two could argue and butt heads with the best of them, but as Lois would always say, "my father loved me so much ... no matter what." Indeed he did, indeed he did. Lois could be a lass off five or six waiting with her dad for the #28 bus out in the bitter cold and snow. There was always her dad to just open that big, long, heavy coat of his and gently guide his little duscha into the warmth and safety of his love.

She could hurt herself climbing over a high fence to play inside a local park. Who would he there to take her to the hospital and make sure all was well? Dad, of course. When his little duscha had grown and went off to the local college, it was her dad that would drive her to school as to ensure her safe arrival.

Pretty does not equal the face of my last wife, Lois. She is a beautiful lady who fills my heart with unmeasured joy. My Lois would have no problem when she was in. Her late teens and early twenties finding herself a date. George would say, "Look at these guys for goodness sake! One has hair like a fuzzy bear and some of the others I'm not nuts over either." George would often say, "I've got a boy for you. How about Roy? He's tall and handsome, comes from a nice family. You two would make a nice couple." Now I must admit that George and I agreed on some things, and not on others. However, on the issue of his "duscha" there is no iota of difference on our feelings for her. After I mustered up the courage to ask Lois out for a date, George took full credit for the relationship that would follow.

Lois grew up to be as fine a person as any who has walked the good Lord's earth. We dated, became engaged, and married on April 20, 1980. By the way, who was there to walk his baby down the aisle? No one else but Dad. A little more than a year later Lois and I were blessed with a baby of our own, a sweet little girl we named Dawn Lisa. Now when Dawn was born, I looked at her in the hospital nursery and I couldn't help myself for saying, "holy cow, it looks like she was in a fight and lost!" Dawn's little nose was positioned near her cheek and her skin was a light shade of yellow. Thank goodness everything centered out within a day. Lois had a long, tough labor with Dawn. So, when I stated to Nana Ethel, Nana Shirley, and Grandpa that we let Lois rest and just visit our new baby, all agreed. Until that is we arrived at the hospital and Grandpa headed directly into his "little duscha's" room. Admittedly, I fumed at the time, but I was naive to think, that he wouldn't be there for Lois, again.

These two, Lois and George, would always joke and tease one another. One of the favorite exchanges between the two concerned driving. Grandpa would say, "You had the best driving teacher, because I taught you how to drive." Lois would shoot back with, "Are you kidding me? If it was up to you I would still be driving inside the Orchard beach parking lot." Grandpa would waste no time when replying, "You weren't ready to go out on the road, you can never be too careful." This story would be bantered about between the two of them countless times.

George was one of those souls who had difficulty making a decision. Not that he didn't make a decision, but he just would take his own sweet time in doing so. I dare say that if Grandpa would have come across a deal for a brand new spanking car that sold for $10,000 and was reduced somehow to $1,000, he would say, "Let's keep looking, we can find a better deal." It's easy to forget, but Grandpa did grow up in the depression era. When if you had two nickels to rub together you were probably better off than the fella's standing next to you. Some habits are harder to break than others and some you can't break at all. When it came to a buck, George knew the full meaning of it and never, ever forgot it either.

Grandpa was blessed with five grandchildren and to all his love was given. No disrespect to any of Richard's children because they are fine young ladies, however, I am just going to relate about Dawn and Andrew, Lois and my children.

Dawn and Grandpa became close and I mean really close. In my opinion, this bond can be attributed to one of the saddest events in any of our lives. Strange that it would seem to happen so, but we lost our Nana Shirley in the spring of 1992. Cancer had beaten her down and stolen her away from all of us much too soon. It was then, the day of her funeral, when all of us were grieving, that Dawny, eleven-years-old, took Grandpa by the hand and did her best to console him. Dawny never left Grandpa's side, never. She stayed by him, gave him love because that was what he needed most. She was a small, but steady presence that would remain with him for the remainder of his days. Dawn was the one, and only one, grandchild that helped Grandpa at both the wake and funeral. Grandpa never forgot this and, as was his way, never failed to mention it time and again.

Dawn would say over the years, "come on Grandpa, sit down by me. I'm going to give you a nice manicure and polish too." Dawn would do this with great glee and Grandpa would respond with great satisfaction, "Hey look at this, that Dawny does some great job!" Dawny and Grandpa, a nice duo those two.

When it came to Andrew, Grandpa didn't know what to think sometimes. One thing he did know and that was he loved him deeply. "What kind of music is he listening to?" Grandpa would often ask with a quizzical expression upon listening to Andrew's style music. Grandpa would reply, "not too pleasant to the ear." Andrew's quick wit and funny sense of humor always kept Grandpa in stitches. "He's very clever, very quick," Grandpa would say. Later, Grandpa would appreciate his only grandson's demeanor. "He's going to be mayor of Suffern someday . . . you just watch and see," Grandpa claimed. Gramps did appreciate Andrew's ability to play the guitar, even if the music was not Sinatra. Andrew also played the saxophone, but not as frequently since his true "passion" became the guitar. "Don't give up the saxophone, that's how you get the girls."

Grandpa would remark. This from a man who proudly stated, "I only had one girlfriend in. my life and I married her!"

Towards the end, when Grandpa became weak and frail, hospitalized and then dependent upon others. This was very devastating to him. During this time my children, our children, Dawn and Andrew were there for him. Many visits came, much love, caring, support and hope was displayed by our children. Dawn's caressing Grandpa, putting lotion on his face, hands and arms; kissing and hugging him. Dawn saying how much she loved him meant the world to George. This act was done quite a few times and for no other reason than love.

Andrew would not, could not be kept away. When home from school, whether it be for a week or a few days, Andrew would always make a point to visit his Grandpa. The two of them would yak it up and laugh at one another as only a grandfather and grandson can. Andrew would bring his razor and shaving cream and give grandpa a nice shave. It was much appreciated and much loved by George. A special touch from a special young man.

In closing, I know that I could probably say many, many things that have taken place over the years, but I just wanted to write fresh ideas before they slowly fade, not all, but I'm sure some.

I would be remiss if I didn't mention Bruce and Donald. Both are Dari's children, she left this world far too early in life. The boys grew up without any parents from the ages nineteen and twenty, having to fend for themselves. Grandpa George, or Uncle George to them became sort of a surrogate Dad. George loved them, cared about them and God knows worried about them. George always considered them his children as well, he kept them, in his heart to his last breath.

To my darling wife, I know that your heart is broken and you feel overwhelming sadness upon you. Please know deep down that the love your Dad had for you and you for him will never die. You were his heart beat, his dear one . . . You were his moya duscha. You took care of him in a way that very few, if any, can, day or night, work or not, you were there for him. You see honey, it came full circle and the long winding road of life came to an end. Always remember the one constant in your Dad's life love and family. For if one has no family, then he has nothing at all. Your dad had family and that means he had it all! So this is not goodbye, nor is it a-final farewell. We love to live and live to love and this will carry us through until we meet again on the other side.

So for now my dear one, it's "Moya Duscha, Moya Duscha."

Your loving husband,
Roy

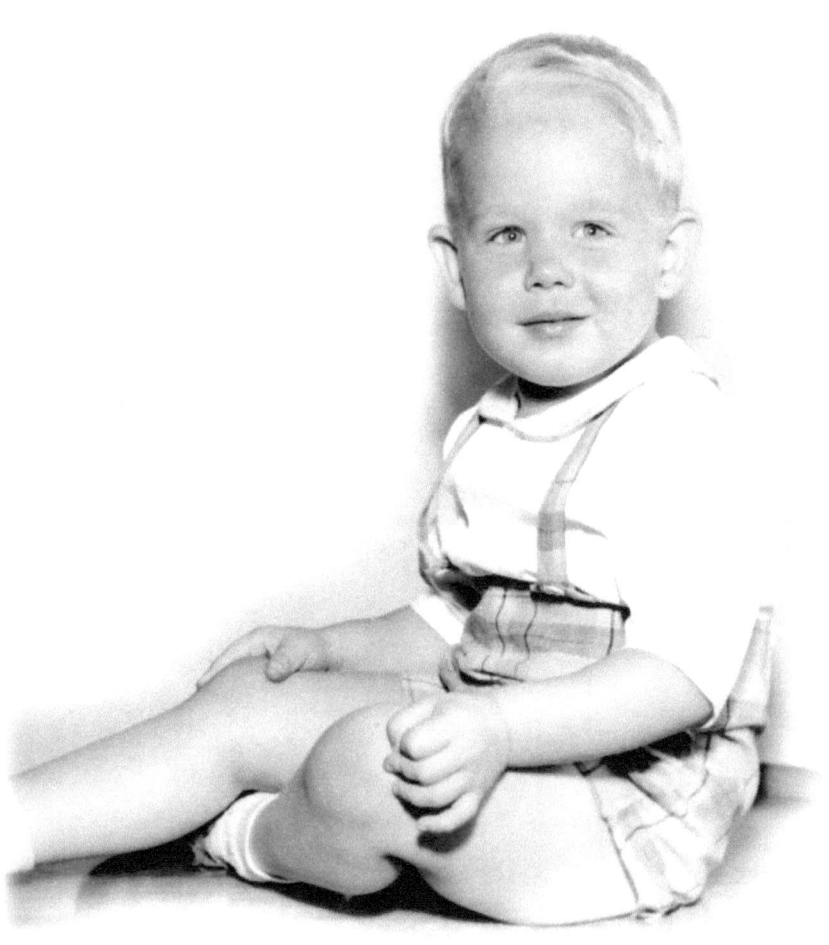

Roy-2 yrs old just startin out!